# Practical Research Methods for Educators

*Becoming an Evidence-Based Practitioner*

**ENNIO CIPANI, PhD**

SPRINGER PUBLISHING COMPANY

New York

Springer Publishing Company, LLC
11 West 42nd Street
New York, NY 10036
www.springerpub.com

*Acquisitions Editor: Philip Laughlin*
*Project Manager: Julia Rosen*
*Cover design: David Levy*
*Composition: Apex CoVantage, LLC*

Ebook ISBN: 978-0-8261-2236-0

09 10 11 12 / 5 4 3 2 1

The author and the publisher of this Work have made every effort to use sources believed to be reliable to provide information that is accurate and compatible with the standards generally accepted at the time of publication. The author and publisher shall not be liable for any special, consequential, or exemplary damages resulting, in whole or in part, from the readers' use of, or reliance on, the information contained in this book. The publisher has no responsibility for the persistence or accuracy of URLs for external or third-party Internet Web sites referred to in this publication and does not guarantee that any content on such Web sites is, or will remain, accurate or appropriate.

---

**Library of Congress Cataloging-in-Publication Data**

Cipani, Ennio.
  Practical research methods for educators : becoming an evidence-based practitioner / Ennio Cipani.
    p. cm.
  Includes bibliographical references and index.
  ISBN 978-0-8261-2235-3 (alk. paper)
  1. Education—Research—Methodology—Textbooks.   I. Title.
  LB1028.C545  2009
  370.7'2—dc22          2009000380

---

Printed in the United States of America by Hamilton Printing

# Contents

# Preface

It would be nice if the material you learned in any course could be demonstrated to be of importance in a future career. I am sure you have been through courses where certain topics that were covered seemed useful, relevant, and functional for your career in education. Of course the converse is also true. There are many topics that seem to have little relevance to what you will be required to know as a teacher in a special day class for elementary students, as a school administrator, as a junior high school math teacher, or in a variety of other positions on the front line of education.

If you are a future elementary school educator, you are probably not required to take a course in tax law or a course in advanced Boolean algebra (although some prospective high school math teachers may be required to take such a course). The relevance of such a course to elementary school teachers would certainly be questionable. It would not serve a functional purpose for the position requirements (although such courses may be of interest to some people).

You are probably taking this course because it is a requirement for a graduate degree that you are seeking. But you may feel that its function for your future career is limited at best and nonexistent at worst. I do not believe that the utility of developing research skills in practitioners is often questioned. The inclusion of a research course in a preparation program for educators is seen as a given. Unfortunately, the skills deemed necessary and desirable often have little practical utility for frontline classroom personnel. For example, many traditional texts on educational research methods written for prospective educational personnel provide extensive treatments of experimental designs that often prove impractical for classroom teachers and school administrators. Should we really expect that teachers will be able to carry out a two by two ($2 \times 2$) group factorial design with random assignment, to determine whether extra phonics practice produces better reading on weekly reading test scores?

If this type of design or methodology is not realistic for practicing teachers, why would a text spend extensive time teaching it, as well as teaching the related statistical tests to analyze that data? While competency with such types of research methodologies and statistical analyses is a skill that an educational researcher working for the Educational Testing Service (ETS) would need to master, this would be overkill (and irrelevant) for current and future classroom practitioners.

I believe this text offers a fresh perspective on developing research skills for educators whose careers will be in the classroom. I believe this text is unique in that it identifies the functional requirements for conducting pragmatic research for everyday instructional personnel. Such a functional approach for future educators is desperately needed. I contend that the development of research skills should focus on two broad objectives for educational personnel who are (or will be) direct line service providers: (1) being producers of applied research that is relevant for classroom practice; and (2) being wise consumers and critics of the research findings reported in literature and everyday conversation.

## BEING PRODUCERS OF APPLIED RESEARCH, RELEVANT FOR CLASSROOM PRACTICE

Not all research is created equal. Some research studies provide answers and solutions to questions and problems relevant to everyday educational practice. Some do not. The distinction between relevant and irrelevant to everyday practice is often seen as the distinction between applied research and basic research. *Applied research* involves testing techniques and procedures that have an effect on classroom behaviors and learning immediately, in a real-life situation. For example, a second-grade teacher would like to use a strategy that helps her students who are just learning the English language to read more words with accuracy and fluency. If a number of teachers have also had difficulty with the reading skills of these students, a need is created for research to address this problem empirically. The findings of such research would be immediately useful to this teacher as well as to teachers who face the same type of problem with English as a Second Language Learners (ELLs).

This teacher is also enrolled in a graduate program in education and feels that this might be a great topic for a thesis. She reviews the research literature and discovers that there are many empirical investigations of this topic. Unfortunately, the overwhelming majority report no experimental data to lend credibility to their assertions. This seems like a great topic for a thesis. After defending her proposal, she initiates the data collection on the dependent variable. She examines each student's scores on weekly 1-minute tests of accuracy and fluency. She collects such data on each student for 10 weeks. During this 10-week period, the ELL students had a 15-minute silent reading time as a strategy to increase accuracy and fluency with grade-level reading materials. Subsequently, upon viewing the results, the teacher verifies the need for improvement across many of the students whose reading accuracy and fluency is below grade level.

What intervention will this teacher use to produce (hopefully) greater reading accuracy and fluency in her ELL students? She has read about peer tutoring and wonders whether such an approach would work in her class. Several studies have demonstrated that peer tutoring is effective in raising oral reading scores, and it seems that using students who read well as peer tutors would be effective. But only the data from such a study would be proof positive. The teacher implements peer tutoring for the last 15 minutes of the class, taking the place of the 15-minute silent-reading period. While some of the articles she had read discussed which approach works best for ELL students, her study will provide evidence. Practitioners of science are concerned with results, not debate. This teacher, being an evidence-based practitioner, will implement and evaluate the efficacy of peer tutoring in her class with each of her ELL students, following the initial experimental condition (i.e., silent reading).

The results over the next 10 weeks confirm the teacher's suspicions. Having her ELL students spend 15 minutes on peer tutoring each day produced a greater number of correct words read per minute (than in the prior 10 weeks) for 80% of the students. Debate is one thing; evidence is another. As you can see, this research study has immediate relevance for this teacher; she learned that 15 minutes of peer tutoring was worth the time invested. While peer tutoring was found to be effective for these students, silent reading was not as effective. The teacher's decision to change the lesson format for the reading period to include peer tutoring is on solid ground. This teacher's applied research answers a question of immediate concern to her. It further validates the teacher's continued use of this strategy as having a solid efficacy base and may provide another study demonstrating the efficacy of peer tutoring with oral reading skills. Just as important, it adds to the research literature on peer tutoring by demonstrating a positive result with ELL students.

In the divergent approach, termed *basic research*, investigators address questions that may not be of immediate utility in real-life situations. Basic research is seen by many as a longitudinal process that may yield application after years of effort have been spent. The intent of the basic researcher is to develop some theory that may explain some aspect of student behavior and/or learning (Gay, Mills, & Airasian, 2006). For example, a basic research study may want to know if the ELL students have more difficulty reading accurately and fluently when they have certain deficits in verbal reasoning. This researcher may have a theory about verbal reasoning as a developmental requisite to reading. Her research will attempt to provide evidence for that theory. She subsequently identifies those students with lower scores on reading measures, as well as those students who have grade-level performance. She then measures their verbal reasoning via one of the commercially available subtests on intelligence measurement. The results illustrate that such students do have lower scores on the verbal reasoning subtest than students who do not have difficulty reading grade-level material in a fluent fashion. But what is the utility of such a finding for the classroom? Get students with higher verbal reasoning scores to enroll in your class? Basic research may or may not lead to application. In the educational arena, the track record of published basic research leading to useful findings is not stellar.

Too often, educational research is not seen as helpful to everyday practitioners. There is a simple explanation for this. Very often, it does not help classroom teachers. This lack of relevance can often create problems for graduate students who intend to conduct their thesis or dissertation in a school district where they are outsiders. Asking a teacher to participate in a research study that does not aid that teacher in educating or managing her classroom more effectively will make it harder to enlist the teacher as a participant. In contrast, asking teachers who have difficulty in getting students to transition more smoothly from one instructional activity to another to participate in a study that will address this problem area would probably be more welcome. The latter study will provide a direct benefit to the teacher(s) if one of the strategies being tested actually works!

Research with applied relevance can also address how to change the behavior of students. A hypothetical elementary grade school has difficulty with students coming in from lunch recess in a timely manner. Would a study that examines student attitudes about school and recess directly solve that problem? No! While such a study might have some information on how students feel about school, the result of conducting this study will not be a change in student tardiness in coming in from lunch recess. In contrast, an applied study might examine several strategies aimed at getting students to line up within 30 seconds of hearing the recess whistle. Suppose the current level of students who line up within 30 seconds is 35%–70% across a 4-week period. If the school tries one strategy, for example, reminding students each day to get in their respective lines within 30 seconds of the recess whistle, then its result on student behavior can be compared against the prior level. If this strategy does not result in a significant improvement, another, more potent technique might be added, for example, loss of recess time for those students not in line at 30 seconds. If the level of students getting in line in a timely fashion now ranges from 60% to 90%, a management problem during recess is solved. With a few additional research design requirements, this data can demonstrate that such an approach, that is, daily reminders and recess fines, results in improved student behavior in this context. Again, the utility of such a finding is immediate, that is, student behavior is improved.

Applied research in education, to be relevant, needs to focus more on empirical tests of interventions and strategies that purportedly produce changes in student behavior and learning. This is particularly evident for those students whose behavior is seen as resistant to typical efforts. What is not helpful in developing a technology of classroom behavior change is conducting a study to survey these students' opinions about their self-esteem. No behavior changes! Nor do we have any evidence that a treatment that could develop increased levels of self-esteem would produce a change in real-life behavior! If the researcher conducting such a study believes that enhancing self-esteem will have an effect on student behavior, prove that directly! Show that an intervention program that produces changes in students' self-esteem results in a change in their test scores, without any confounding interpretation. We need fewer studies that show associations and more studies that show treatment effects directly.

## BEING WISE CONSUMERS AND CRITICS OF RESEARCH FINDINGS

A physician who treats persons with various heart problems relies on research, in the form of clinical trials, to determine which treatment regimens to administer to her patients. She must keep abreast of the research findings with respect to the statins (a drug class for treating high cholesterol) that have been found to be effective with patients and present the fewest risks in terms of side effects. Her use of these drugs is based on a rigorous research program demonstrating that such a drug will lower cholesterol levels in patients with such medical presenting problems. A practicing physician does not rely on evidence that does not demonstrate an effect on the criterion variable, in this case, the cholesterol levels of patients. Medical personnel have been evidence-based practitioners for years. Theories are not evidence! But how does this relate to the use of teaching and management approaches in classrooms?

As someone who is about to enter (or has entered) the profession of education, how often have you heard someone use "the research says . . ." to bolster his or her argument for implementing some procedure, strategy, or policy? Very often, such statements are not challenged. Yet it may be questionable whether there is research that demonstrates the efficacy of such a procedure. Here is a great example.

*Is there really a memory pill?* There are many products on the market claiming that they improve memory. They often claim that there is clinical research demonstrating that memory is improved. But the devil is in the details. Here are some hypothetical research studies claiming that the results support the daily use of a particular memory pill as a treatment that improves people's memory:

- Charts, developed by scientists, that show how this pill affects neurotransmitter substances in the brain
- MRI scans that show increased blood flow in the brain after a group of participants have been using the memory pill for 6 weeks
- Correlations between blood flow in the brain and short-term memory (measured by tests)
- Data from participants taking the pill reporting that they felt it improved their memory
- Testimonials from actors about their use of the memory pill, reporting an improved ability to remember their lines
- Results demonstrating that gains in memory (as measured by a test) were attained by participants using the pill for a prescribed period of time and that such gains were not obtained with a group of participants who were given a placebo pill (where the members of neither group were aware of which pill they were getting)

Which of the above studies constitute empirical evidence regarding the efficacy of a memory pill in improving the memory? None! Did you fall for the charts on neurotransmitters and the information on blood flow as evidence that memory pills produce a better memory? Such studies would require a *leap of faith* to accept the theory that increasing blood flow to the brain will result in better memory. It did not demonstrate that such a result actually occurred. It showed that the pill produces changes in blood flow (that is verified) but failed to take the next step, which means demonstrating that such a result in the brain leads to a change in memory ability (by actually measuring the change).

*Brain research has to be credible!* What about a study demonstrating that people who have greater blood flow in the brain do better on memory tests than people who show less blood flow. Does the study show that a product that can increase blood flow will improve memory? No, it does not! It may be the case that increasing blood flow will result in better test results, but that part of the experiment was not conducted! Again it requires a leap of faith. To demonstrate the treatment efficacy of the pill, it would have required that the researchers follow up such a study with a clinical trials study involving people with poor memories (and presumably less blood flow). If the researchers then demonstrate, with those participants, that increasing the blood flow results in changes in memory, then such a study provides empirical evidence.

As a practitioner in education, you will often be confronted by people who say "the research says . . . ." After this course, you will respond with, "Show me the data!" You will be able to critically evaluate whether the conclusion they are drawing is warranted. If they can produce experimental data, demonstrating that some variable causes a change in student behavior, you will see that their conclusions are warranted. If their research findings require a leap of faith, you will now be able to spot that. You can inform them that they do not have the necessary evidence regarding the efficacy of their theory or approach.

*Don't be fooled!* Suppose a group of "experts" develop a theory that the most effective manner of developing reading skills in young children is to use a multisensory method and approach. They reason that if children listen to stories (providing auditory sensation), then draw pictures about the stories (providing a visual sensory component), and finally mime the story for a peer, reading scores will improve. These experts get testimonials from reading teachers who agree that such an innovative strategy for teaching reading decoding and comprehension would no doubt work. The experts conduct a survey and find that 90%

of the reading specialists surveyed scored the approach as either certainly efficacious or probably efficacious. Does this constitute empirical evidence that this approach is effective? Only if scientific knowledge is acquired by conducting Gallup polls! The leap of faith is that the results of a future study would parallel the survey data. In contrast, readers of this book will not accept such a leap of faith but require studies demonstrating that the approach under consideration results in better reading test scores than other approaches.

## OVERVIEW OF THE TEXT

This text begins by presenting the scientific method in chapter 1. The reader is given a basic discussion of the measurement of two specific variables: the dependent variable and the independent variable. The chapter covers three basic forms of research: descriptive, correlation, and experimental. The chapter will target the skills necessary for the practitioner to become a wise consumer of research findings. The remaining chapters will then build the skills needed to conduct applied research in classrooms.

Chapter 2 provides detail on the requisites for single-case research and on its methodological designs. Three characteristics of single-case designs are delineated. Chapter 3 presents information on measuring the dependent variable in single-case research studies. The sine qua non of measurement in applied research is a direct measurement of behavior. Issues of reliability and validity are presented next. The rest of the chapter then focuses on steps to measuring behavior and learning as the primary dependent measures used in single-case research designs.

Chapter 4 presents a variety of single-case designs for use in classroom research projects. For each design, the chapter presents a brief description of the design, some figures illustrating the research design features with hypothetical data, and some research studies that have utilized such a design. Each type of single-case design is discussed with regard to its advantages and limitations in demonstrating cause-and-effect relationships.

Chapter 5 provides a discussion of the four types of applied research that can be conducted: demonstration, comparative, parametric, and component analysis. The remainder of this chapter provides a variety of possible examples of applied research with respect to a number of behavioral and instructional interventions and looks at how the four types of studies could be conducted. Chapter 5 presents a discussion of types of applied research and a host of potential research areas.

## REFERENCE

Gay, L. R., Mills, G. E., & Airasian, P. (2006). *Educational research: Competencies for analysis and applications* (8th ed.). Columbus, OH: Merrill/Prentice Hall.

# 1  Science and the Scientific Method

## WHAT IS SCIENCE?

Science is the systematic study of phenomena to gain knowledge about the world. Scientists have two core sets of beliefs: (1) a belief in determinism, and (2) a belief in empiricism rather than speculation as a means of gaining knowledge (Cooper, Heron, & Heward, 2007). This chapter reviews the basic premises of science and shows how different research methodologies provide the mechanism for collecting different types of knowledge.

## Belief in Determinism

Do you believe that phenomena occur randomly (accidentalism) or that events are the result of a combination of occurrences leading to a result (determinism; Cooper et al., 2007)? Scientists generally subscribe to determinism. For example, if you believe in determinism, you will view changes in the weather as a function of changes in certain weather events. Your explanation for hurricanes and their strength (Categories 1–5) will rely on an analysis of certain weather and oceanic variables that set the conditions under which hurricanes form. The degree to which meteorologists better understand how such variables impact weather makes them more capable of predicting weather patterns and hurricane strength during the summer months in the Caribbean and the Atlantic Ocean.

If you do not believe that a combination of certain levels of relevant variables affects weather conditions, then you will see events such as hurricanes as unpredictable. This approach might best be called "weather happens." You will be inclined to believe that the weather on one day will have no effect on the next day's weather. Given our society's sophistication with explanations of what variables influence weather patterns, a deterministic view is very plausible in understanding weather. However, centuries ago, the explanation offered for weather events relied on some aspect of a deity.

In education, determinism as a philosophical position views environmental and inheritable characteristics as variables that explain behavior. Of course, to educators, environmental variables are more relevant. Environmental variables can be studied and potentially altered to produce desired changes in the rate of behavior and level of academic performance. Determinism in education can be characterized by the adage "Teaching (method) matters!" If learning were a function of random events, then teaching would become irrelevant. One would just wait for "it" (i.e., student learning) to happen. When we are lucky, students learn. When we are unlucky, they do not. In contrast, a belief that what we do as teachers affects learners (in both desired and undesired directions) requires a belief that learner behavior is determined in some part or in large part by environmental conditions.

## Belief in Empiricism

Where is the evidence? For scientists, knowing something (knowledge) requires reliable and valid evidence. Consider this statement: This child's behavior is driven by an innate desire to be good. The statement speculates that the child's behavior is a function of an innate desire. But how would you measure any child's innate desire? Further, how would a contention such as the one presented above be proven? If you were able to derive a reliable and valid method of measuring a child's innate desire, you would then have to demonstrate this relationship. Subsequently, you would have to show that children who have this innate desire behave in one manner and children who do not possess such a desire behave in another (in some quantitative manner). If this sounds a lot like "The id made me do it!" you now see that explanations of human behavior have evolved from speculative to empirical in the last half century (at least among the majority of professional people).

Empiricism is based on an objective, quantitative measurement of a phenomenon of interest (Cooper et al., 2007). Such a measurement must be demonstrated to be free from the bias of the researchers (Cooper et al., 2007). Scientific findings obtained via an empirical approach are neither good nor bad but value free. Demonstrating that a nuclear reaction occurs when nuclear particles are made to collide with each other is a fact of science. That fact is neither positive nor negative but a matter of empirical demonstration. How people use such knowledge becomes a social value issue.

In an empirical approach, experimentation is the vehicle for gaining knowledge about the world. We learn about a phenomenon by subjecting it to study. Further, to develop a knowledge base, a number of studies related to the phenomenon must be conducted (Sidman, 1960). Replication of results with additional studies is essential because one finding alone does not make a law of nature! If an empirical study is truly devoid of the personal bias of the experimenter, other researchers should be able to replicate the findings, as long as the variables are measured in the same manner as they were in the original study. Experimentation may demonstrate either that two variables covary or that one variable can cause changes in the other.

## SCIENCE AND THE STUDY OF VARIABLES

### Questions to Ponder

- If you were interested in knowing whether students learn better with cooperative learning, what other condition(s) would have to be tested?
- What is the relationship between the dependent variable and the independent variable?

## What Is a Variable?

A variable is a phenomenon that varies along some quantitative measure (Matheson, Bruce, & Beauchamp, 1978). For example, if you are told that your child's weight can vary on a given day by up to 2 pounds, depending on the time of day, this means that your child's weight is variable across time. However, if you are told that his or her weight at 3:20 p.m. was

112 pounds, then that measure is not variable (rather, it is a constant). In other words, a variable varies in quantity over a number of circumstances. Examine the statements in the left hand column of Table 1.1 to determine whether a variable or a constant is implied.

## Two Major Variables: One Depends on the Other

Scientific inquiry is concerned with two major variables: the dependent variable and the independent variable. The *dependent variable* exemplifies its name: Its value depends on another variable (the independent variable). Remember in basic algebra class you were often asked to plot a linear equation, such as $y = 3x + 5$, on an $x$, $y$ coordinate graph. If I ask you, "What is the value of $y$ in that equation?" what would be your answer? "It depends!" And you would be right! The value of $y$ depends on the value you assign to $x$. If $x$ is given a value of 2, what is the value of $y$? Eleven. We can change the value of $y$ simply by changing the value of $x$. When $x$ is given a value of 3, the value of $y$ becomes 14, as the value of $y$ varies with the change in the value assigned to $x$. The value of $y$ depends on the assigned value of $x$. In contrast, the equation $y = 3$ does not vary; hence it is not a variable but a constant.

Table 1.1

### WHICH OF THE FOLLOWING?

| STATEMENT | VARIABLE (YES/NO) |
|---|---|
| The length of your right foot at 9:00 on May 25, 2009 | No, one value |
| The shoe sizes of residents of Cocoa Beach, Florida | Yes, many values (Cocoa Beach has more than one resident) |
| The number of times you scold your dog each day for a 1-month period (let's assume you have a dog) | Yes |
| The square footage of your house/apartment | No, exact amount |
| The time it takes you to run 100 meters in four consecutive races | Yes, variation across four different races |
| The length of time you spend texting your friends each day for 1 week | Yes |

In applied educational research, the dependent variables of interest are concerned with student behavior (often called the *criterion variable* in relationship studies). In this context, the study of student behavior refers to any measure of student behavior or performance. Examples of student behavior can be any of the following: the number of student disruptive incidents in a cafeteria period, the number of positive comments made by one student to another, or the number of plastic bottles recycled during lunch periods. Student performance can be measured in any of the following ways: test scores, the number of items correct on assignments, or the length and sophistication of expository writing samples.

The *independent variable* is the phenomenon that the researcher manipulates, and whose effect on student behavior or performance the researcher studies. In education, four main types of independent variables often studied in experimental research are the following: (1) type of learning materials, (2) instructional method, (3) reinforcement contingencies, and (4) length of instruction/treatment (Gay, Mills, & Airasian, 2006). Suppose a researcher is interested in studying the effects of several different learning materials on student learning. Since the independent variable must vary, one has to specify at least two conditions (or levels) of the learning-materials variable. It is insufficient to simply implement one method and study the effect on student performance. Why? Because the independent variable does not vary in that circumstance: it is constant. However, if you have two sets of learning materials, say, Math Curriculum A and Math Curriculum B, you now have variation. Consequently, you can now study how that variation in the independent variable affects student performance. In other words, what happens to student performance when Curriculum A is in effect versus when Math Curriculum B is in effect? Does student performance vary significantly as a function of which of these two sets of materials is in place? This study would be given the following title: "The effect of two different types of curriculum material on student math scores measuring 10 instructional objectives."

A research study will often delineate in its title the two variables studied. Table 1.2 gives the titles of two hypothetical research studies. The dependent variable is underlined, while the independent variable is italicized.

In the first study, the independent variable, number of rehearsal items with feedback, will vary at least over two levels. One level could be 3 student rehearsal items with feedback per lesson, while another

Table 1.2

---

**DEPICTION OF DEPENDENT AND INDEPENDENT VARIABLES**

1. *The effects of number of rehearsal items with feedback* on 11th-grade students' acquisition of the skill of computing correct values for two variables in a linear system
2. *The effects of rule reminders* on student compliance with classroom rules during teacher lecture in a 2nd-year Spanish class

---

level could be 10 items with feedback per level. Both these conditions will be evaluated against the 11th-grade students' performance on math items measuring the solving of unknowns in a linear system. In the second study, the effects of rule reminders on the level of student compliance with classroom rules will be assessed. This will again require that the independent variable will have at least two levels, for example, daily reminders from the teacher about the classroom rules versus weekly lectures about the rules.

Scientific inquiry has three basic purposes, from which are derived three basic methods of science. The three basic purposes are as follows: (1) describe the phenomenon; (2) examine relationships between variables; and (3) determine cause-and-effect relationships (via manipulating experimentally relevant variables). The types of research studies for each of these purposes are descriptive research, correlation research, and experimental research, respectively. The remainder of this chapter will present each of the methods that are used to uncover such information.

## DESCRIPTIVE RESEARCH STUDIES

### Questions to Ponder
- Can a descriptive study determine what causes student behavior? Why or why not?
- Would a descriptive study be indicated if one wanted to determine how many second-grade students can memorize a 3-minute song in one 30-minute training session?
- What are the differences between descriptive observational research and survey research?

- Why is it not acceptable to make generalizations about actual student behavior from survey research?
- Why is a descriptive observational research study unable to reach conclusions on cause-and-effect relationships?

## Descriptive Observational Research

Description is perhaps the easiest form of gaining knowledge and a first step toward subsequent scientific inquiry. You simply watch a phenomenon and describe what you observe. This is termed descriptive observational research. Suppose you wanted to learn more about ants. If you are a scientist, you would have to come in contact with ants in order to directly study and observe their patterns of behavior. It would be inappropriate to speculate about ants because you have had experience with frogs, birds, or other animals. You would first identify where ants live, to allow for direct observation. You would then possibly observe these ants for some period of time. You would begin to look for patterns of ant behavior and begin to come up with hypotheses about ant activities. A descriptive study would then possibly measure the frequency or duration of certain patterns of ant behaviors in relation to other events. In contrast to other methods of science, you simply describe the behavior of the ants without altering their environment in any way.

In descriptive research, observation of the phenomenon is conducted by the researcher. It is essential to obtain a recording of the observation(s) that allows for quantification. A quantifiable method of collecting information from observations of behavior separates a more scientific approach from a simple anecdotal record. If you have a hypothesis about the existence of a certain phenomenon in an educational setting, your first step would be to collect information that describes that phenomenon. A descriptive study would then measure that phenomenon, in a quantitative manner. Such data would then allow you to determine whether your hypothesis is accurate.

What would be an example of a descriptive observational study with children? Suppose an educational researcher speculates that children who engage in disruptive behavior during the lunch recess are often not disciplined. This researcher translates the area of inquiry into the following research question: How often are consequences (i.e., discipline) deployed for children who engage in disruptive behavior during lunch recess? This research question can be addressed by collecting data on two phenomena. First, the researcher observes the number of times children engage in disruptive behavior during lunch recess. Second, the researcher also measures how often consequences (delineated a priori) are levied shortly after each disruptive incident. If the rate of consequences following an act of disruptive behavior is 10% (meaning that 90% of the time no consequences are delivered following the act), this researcher's hypothesis is confirmed. Table 1.3 provides hypothetical data on the percentage of times disruptive behavior results in the utilization of at least one of three identified consequences over a 5-day period.

This hypothetical study merely describes how often consequences (from the list of three measured by the researcher) befall acts of disruptive behavior during lunch recess. The percentage of times that consequences were deployed ranged from a low of 20% to a high of 50% of the times when disruptive behavior occurred. This study cannot address any question related to the effects of one variable (consequences or lack thereof) on the other (rate of disruptive behavior). Descriptive observational research simply describes conditions (in a quantitative fashion) as they currently exist.

A study conducted by a group of researchers at Valdosta State University sought to determine whether the rate of correct responses was different during initial instruction (i.e., new material) than during practice lessons (Gunter, Reffel, Barnett, Lee, & Patrick, 2004). Three observers collected data on correct response rates in 104 elementary classrooms from seven schools. During 5-minute observations in a given classroom, the observer marked whether the academic question was taken from new instructional material (initial instruction) or from previously reviewed

Table 1.3

| DESCRIPTIVE ANALYSIS DATA | | | | | |
|---|---|---|---|---|---|
| | **DATE** | | | | |
| | **MARCH 2** | **MARCH 3** | **MARCH 4** | **MARCH 5** | **MARCH 6** |
| Frequency of acts of disruptive behavior | 10 | 20 | 12 | 15 | 10 |
| Frequency a consequence followed an act of disruptive behavior | 4 | 10 | 4 | 3 | 4 |
| Percentage of times consequences were deployed | 40% | 50% | 33% | 20% | 40% |

material (practice lesson). Correct responses were then marked for each individual student answer. In order for correct responses to be recorded when a group choral response was made, 80% of the students' answers had to be correct. The median correct response rate for initial instruction was 2.8, while the review or practice lessons resulted in a median correct response rate of 4.1 (which was statistically significant). While such data reveal naturalistic rates of such behavior across many classrooms, they do not provide the effect of this variable (initial versus review lessons) on student acquisition of material (e.g., probe test data). The mechanism lacking in descriptive observational studies that precludes causal analysis is the failure to actively manipulate one of the variables, that is, the independent variable. This translates to an inability to determine cause-and-effect relationships, irrespective of how compelling the obtained observational data are.

## Survey Research

Survey data often falls into the category of descriptive research. Survey research gathers the opinions of the survey respondents and presents these data in a summary form. Conducting a survey study that examines how many students with attention deficit hyperactivity disorder (ADHD) ingest above-average levels of sugar would be an example of a descriptive study using survey data. Each student with ADHD participating in the study would possibly fill out a questionnaire about his or her sugar intake. The survey could have the students check off the category that best describes his or her sugar intake. This category system allows the researcher to determine for each respondent whether daily sugar intake is below, at, or above the usual levels of intake.

The results would merely report the percentage of students sampled whose intake of sugar exceeded some designated level (in the category of above-average intake). The finding might be that 50% of the students with ADHD sampled reported daily sugar intake that was above that consumed by other students. When such data are collected by surveying the intended participants (either verbally or using paper and pencil), it is termed survey research.

Survey research contrasts with descriptive observational research in that the criterion variable is measured indirectly. The sugar intake study with students with ADHD could be turned into an observational study by changing the data collection method. If the researcher collects data by observing these students and measuring their sugar intake directly, it becomes a descriptive observational study. Hypothetically, the researcher may observe these students at lunch time, recording whether they eat a candy bar or drink soda for lunch. She may then report that 70% of her sample of students with ADHD ate up to one candy bar during lunch (allowing for not finishing it), while 35% of those observed ate more than one candy bar at lunch. Note that such a study does not identify what effect such activities may have (although the author may want you to take a leap of faith and infer what the effect would be). It simply describes a phenomenon.

## Conducting a Descriptive Research Study

Conducting a descriptive observational study is relatively straightforward in terms of the data collection process (see Table 1.4). Direct observation of the phenomenon is required. Selection of the variable(s) to measure via observation is an early decision in the research process.

## Utility of Descriptive Studies for Educational Practitioners

Descriptive studies that entail the collection of survey data do not contribute significantly to identifying effective intervention techniques for behavioral and educational learning problems. First, the accuracy and reliability of self-report survey data is very suspect. Can one trust that what people say in a survey reflects what their response would be a week from the time they filled out the questionnaire?

Table 1.4

### STEPS TO CONDUCTING A DESCRIPTIVE OBSERVATIONAL STUDY

1. Delineate the variable(s) you are interested in, and how these will be measured.
2. Define the group of students who will be involved in the data collection process and the setting for the study.
3. Measure the student or environmental variable in a quantitative fashion across the students from the designated setting.
4. Collect the data for a period of time to achieve some stable measure of the variable being measured.
5. Report the data in some usable form, for example, frequency, percentage, and so forth.

Second, the assumption that opinion data provide insight into effective strategies is flawed. Survey data reporting that 85% of dentists prefer a brand of toothpaste with a licorice taste do not translate to a finding that licorice is an effective component in toothpaste. Consensus, even at high levels, does not provide scientific evidence that something works under certain conditions. Similarly, finding that most teachers who are judged to be great teachers prefer to use mild discipline approaches when dealing with behavior problems does not validate such approaches. *A Gallup poll, even with a sample of people judged to be great at their craft, does not equate to a science of cause-and-effect with respect to student behavior.* Could it be that great teachers may have great students? In that case, how can the finding help teachers who have less-than-great students?

Descriptive observational studies can have some value in initially exploring some classroom phenomena. However, descriptive observational research does not allow for an analysis of cause-and-effect. Describing a phenomenon, while possibly useful in determining the extent to which a phenomenon occurs, does not provide any direction for solving any observed problem(s). Cause-and-effect analysis can only be derived from a research methodology that actively manipulates the independent variable and assesses the effect on the dependent variable.

## CORRELATION RESEARCH STUDIES

### Questions to Ponder
- Why do correlation studies not allow for causal conclusions? What would a study have to demonstrate for one to conclude that a difference in teaching strategy caused changes in student learning?
- Explain why a correlation coefficient of −.77 indicates a strong relationship between two variables. Given this negative correlation, would high scores on the predictor variable translate to high or low scores on the criterion variable?
- What would be the danger of inferring cause from a correlation study showing that eating more peanut butter is statistically related to better student performance in the first two periods of the school day? In other words, what would be the danger if, as a result of this correlation finding, schools start asking all students to start eating peanut butter in the morning?

- What does an inverse correlation coefficient illustrate between two variables, *a* and *b*? Describe what happens to the values on variable *a* when the values on variable *b* decrease.
- Does a correlation coefficient of .90 depict a cause-and-effect relationship between two variables? Why or why not?

## Examining the Relationship Between Two Variables

In educational and psychological research, studies often measure two or more variables, without any experimental manipulation, and attempt to determine whether there is a relationship (or association) between them. A relationship exists between two variables when knowing the value of one variable allows you to estimate, to some degree, what the value would be of the other variable. Here is a simple, more concrete example using two variables, labeled *x* and *y*. We begin by measuring these two variables across 10 circumstances. We measure the variable called *x* across these 10 circumstances. We also measure the variable called *y* across these same 10 circumstances. We find that the value of *y* is always two times the value of *x* (remember basic algebraic equations: $y = 2x$). When *x* is 4, the value of *y* is 8. When *x* is 12, *y* is 24. In that scenario, we would have a direct linear relationship and perfect prediction. If someone tells you the value of *x* (called the *predictor variable*), you can predict what the value of *y* (called the *criterion variable*) is. While research on human behavior is not perfect in regard to prediction, educational and psychological researchers try to discern which variables correlate with student variables such as achievement, performance, and/or behavior. Provided the two variables are quantified, you can study the extent of the relationship between them.

When two events covary with high probability, prediction becomes possible. If height predicts weight to some degree, one could give a reasonable estimate of weight given height. For example, if someone is over 6 feet 2 inches tall, would you guess that she or he would weigh less than 120 pounds? Probably not. And 999 out of 1,000 times you would be right.

Suppose we hypothesize that getting to school on time is a predictor of school success. You select a number of children to observe and from whom to obtain data on how often they are late to school over a period of time. Some children get to school on time every day. Other children may be late 1 or 2 days a week. Maybe some other children are late 4 or 5 days a week. Based on attendance data that is collected across 20 weeks within the academic year, each student is identified as belonging to one of three categories: (1) frequently late, (2) sometimes late, or (3) infrequently late. Students are classified as frequently late if the mean number of days late per week is between 3.0 and 5. Students whose mean number of days of being late to school is between 1.0 and 2.9 are classified as sometimes late. Finally, students whose mean number of days of being late to school is less than 1.0 are classified as infrequently late. Once you have gathered such data, you would then determine whether the level of getting to school on time is associated with school success. For the purposes of this hypothetical example, we could define school success as each student's test score on a standardized reading achievement test.

Now that we have quantifiable measures on the two variables of interest, we can determine how related these variables are. Let's say the results depict the following: Students who are in the infrequently late category are also the students with the highest reading comprehension test scores. Concurrently, those who are in the frequently late category generally have the lowest scores. Given these data, the results illustrate that the two variables covary. Knowing something about a student in terms of school arrival times allows you to estimate (with some degree of accuracy) the student's reading achievement test score. If I told you there is a student entering the third grade who is late 4 to 5 days per week, what would you guess is his or her reading score? You would guess it is low. If the strength of the correlation between these two variables is very high, your guess has a very good chance of being correct.

## Correlation Research Addresses Degree of Association

Correlation research addresses two questions (Cohen, Manion, & Morrison, 2003, p. 193). First, is there a relationship between two (or more) variables of interest? Second, what is the direction and what is the magnitude of the relationship? Correlation research involves proving that some variable covaries with a more complex variable (the dependent variable).

Correlation studies are frequently used to develop or build theories about child behavior and performance. Here is a hypothetical example. A researcher believes (i.e., has a theory) that getting plenty of sleep is related to better school performance for children with ADHD. In attempting to gather evidence that such a theory may be accurate, she decides to conduct a study testing the relationship between the two variables.

This researcher specifies the population of interest as children with ADHD. She obtains a sample of participants who are hopefully representative of this population (children with ADHD), as her theory must have broad application to children with ADHD in general. She selects 120 high school students with ADHD, from 25 school districts, as the participants for her study. She defines school performance as each student's test scores on two midterm tests. This allows her to measure school performance in a quantitative manner, for example, using midterm scores in spelling and math (two dependent variables). To measure sleep levels, she develops a survey. She has the students fill out this survey, giving information about the amount of sleep they get over a 3-week period (self-report data). If sleep length is related to performance (as measured by weekly test grades), then one would see higher test scores for those students who report more hours of sleep each night. Students who score poorly on the tests would be the ones who report fewer hours of sleep per night. As you can see (Table 1.5), generally, the more hours of sleep a student reports he or she gets, the higher the test scores. Conversely, the fewer hours of sleep a student reports he or she gets, the lower the test scores in spelling and math (first nine participants depicted).

Table 1.5

**RAW DATA FOR TEST SCORES AND AVERAGE NUMBER OF HOURS SLEEP PER NIGHT**

| PARTICIPANT NO. | AVERAGE NO. HOURS SLEEP/DAY | TEST GRADE MATH | TEST GRADE SPELLING |
|---|---|---|---|
| 1 | 8.25 | 82% | 90% |
| 2 | 4.75 | 50% | 35% |
| 3 | 6.0 | 50% | 50% |
| 4 | 7.75 | 76% | 81% |
| 5 | 3.75 | 40% | 60% |
| 6 | 9.0 | 95% | 88% |
| 7 | 6.0 | 70% | 60% |
| 8 | 8.5 | 100% | 100% |
| 9 | 5.5 | 60% | 70% |

## Magnitude of Association: The Correlation Coefficient

In this hypothetical researcher's sample, it seems that higher levels of self-reported sleep covary with test performance. But what is the magnitude of the relationship in the above study? Is sleep highly correlated with test grades, or is the relationship fairly weak? The determination of this is quantitative. You simply do not look at the raw data sets and proclaim a strong relationship. Rather, correlation research expresses the magnitude of the relationship between the two variables as a correlation coefficient.

A correlation coefficient ranges from –1.0 to +1.0. Correlations of 1.0 and –1.0 are perfect and could be expressed by a linear equation ($y = 3x + 17$, or $y = -3x + 17$). Knowing the value of $x$ (number of hours of sleep) yields only one $y$ value (test score on math or reading). Correlations of less than 1.0, or greater than –1.0, demonstrate a relationship that is less than perfect. The further away from these two endpoints the correlation coefficient is, the weaker the relationship between the two variables. When an association (relationship) is strong between two variables, the correlation coefficient is closer to 1.0 or to –1.0. A correlation coefficient of .78 demonstrates a stronger relationship between the two variables than a coefficient of .50.

For example, let us say that our hypothetical researcher found that the correlation coefficient between sleep and test performance was .80 for math and .73 for spelling. Such a finding indicates a strong relationship between these two achievement test score variables. With this strong a relationship for both math and spelling, knowing the level of reported sleep allows us to speculate what test performance is. If a correlation coefficient of .45 was obtained for the math test score only, it indicates a moderate relationship. We would be less capable of predicting a student's test score on math knowing his or her level of sleep per night.

You might be surprised to learn that a correlation coefficient of –1.0 translates to a model of perfect prediction, since it involves a negative correlation. A correlation coefficient of –1.0 indicates a perfect inverse relationship. An inverse relationship (also called a negative direction) means that high scores on one variable result in lower scores on the other (i.e., the inverse of a positive direction). Suppose the researcher had obtained a strong negative correlation between sleep and test scores. The prediction of test scores given sleep patterns would be the inverse of what was stipulated above for a positive correlation. If a correlation coefficient of –.80 was obtained for math and a coefficient of –.90 for spelling, the following relationship can be detected for both test scores: The more sleep a student gets, the lower the test performance. Conversely, the less sleep he or she gets, the higher the test scores. To reiterate, with negative correlations of sufficient magnitude, high scores on one variable predict lower scores on the other variable.

In summary, a correlation coefficient is the degree to which the collected data fit into a linear equation, that is, a straight line. A more useful statistic is produced when you square the correlation coefficient (i.e., you multiply it by itself). The resulting statistic is called $r^2$. This statistic, $r^2$, depicts the percentage of common or shared variance between the two variables. For example, a correlation coefficient of .90 depicts a strong positive correlation between two variables. To obtain the percentage of common variance, you square it, multiplying .9 by .9, thus getting .81 or 81%. Using this example, the obtained relationship depicts a large amount of shared variance between these two variables. It means that 81% of the variance in the data sets is accounted for by the relationship between reported levels of sleep and test scores. Conversely, 19% of the variation is unaccounted for, meaning the scores are accounted for by some unknown (unmeasured) predictor variable.

Table 1.6 presents correlation coefficients that are hierarchically arranged from strong to weak relationships between two variables, providing the percentage of common variance in the second column.

## Table 1.6

### EXAMPLES OF CORRELATION COEFFICIENTS AND SHARED VARIANCE

| CORRELATION COEFFICIENT ($r$) | COMMON OR SHARED VARIANCE ($r^2$) | |
|---|---|---|
| .95 | $.95^2 = 90\%$ | Strong relationship—much common variance |
| −.92 | $−.92^2 = 85\%$ | Note that negative correlations still indicate strong relationships between two variables |
| .77 | $.77^2 = 59\%$ | Note the drop in common variance when the correlation coefficient is lower |
| −.31 | $−.31^2 = 10\%$ | Little common variance |
| .20 | $−.20^2 = 4\%$ | Negligible common variance |
| .09 | $−.09^2 = $ less than 1% | Virtually no relationship; one score cannot provide you with any idea about a score on another variable |

A rough framework for assessing the strength of a relationship between two variables on the basis of the correlation coefficient (irrespective of sign) is as follows: (1) correlations between 0.00 and .35 are low, (2) correlations between .35 and .65 are moderate, and (3) correlations above .65 are strong (Gay et al., 2006).

Many correlation studies use already existing (archival) data on two or more variables. This merely requires the researcher to compile the data sets across the participants of the study and then subject this to statistical analysis. For example, studying the effects of early intervention on the social development of kindergarten students with developmental disabilities would attempt to find out if a relationship exists between receiving early intervention and social development. The researcher would identify two groups of kindergartners with disabilities, those who received early intervention and those who did not receive it. Some measure of social development would already be in existence. This data would be regressed against the variable of early intervention (dichotomous variable). These types of studies have been referred to as causal-comparative studies, although the term causal is a misnomer. One cannot infer cause and effect from any study whose methodology did not experimentally manipulate the independent variable.

## Conducting a Correlation Study

Conducting correlation research is relatively straightforward in terms of the data collection process (see Table 1.7). Very often, such studies use data that is already existent (called archival data). Selection of the variables that you believe are related and the pool of participants from which to extract the data set is an early decision in the research process.

## Utility of Correlation Studies for Classroom Practice

Prediction studies can be useful where there is a high correlation between predictor variables and some criterion you want to predict. Formulas that determine a person's creditworthiness are used to make judgments about loans and the amount of the loans. It would be silly to simply "go with your gut" when dealing with hundreds of thousands of dollars in prime loans for residential or commercial buildings. Correlation coefficients and prediction models allow the user to possibly predict (with some minimal level of error) what score you would get on one variable by knowing another. Using such predictor models allows people in decision-making positions

Table 1.7

## STEPS TO CONDUCTING A CORRELATION STUDY

■ Delineate the two variables you believe are associated with the population of interest (one of the variables being relevant for student learning behavior).

■ Define the group of students who will be included in the data collection process.

■ Measure the student variable in a quantitative fashion across many students from the designated sample representing the population of interest; if the measurement has already been performed, extract the data from archives.

■ Define the other variable (instructional approach, teacher behaviors or characteristics, school characteristics, and so forth).

■ Measure, in a quantitative fashion, that variable or those variables if it is a multivariate study.

■ Subject the set of data to a statistical test that determines the degree to which the student variable is related to the teacher or school variable, called a correlation coefficient.

■ Determine whether the obtained coefficient indicates a strong relationship by determining if the result is statistically significant (e.g., at the .05 alpha level of significance).

to make fewer errors in judgment. In an another example, college admissions departments at major universities try to use certain predictor variables in determining whether a high school graduate would be successful in a particular college program.

However, there is a major caveat to correlation research and its utility for classroom practice. No matter how high the correlation is between the two variables, one cannot conclude that a cause-and-effect relationship exists. Correlation research does not allow for an analysis of cause and effect. For example, let us say that the hypothetical study referred to above finds that sleep level is positively related to school performance. In other words, the larger the amount of reported sleep, the higher the test scores of students with ADHD. Does that mean this researcher proved that getting more sleep will make someone get better test grades? While it may be tempting to make such a claim, this conclusion goes beyond the research methodology and resulting data. It requires a leap of faith. An alternative causal explanation could be that better school performance may cause better sleep. Or possibly another variable, number of hours spent studying, causes both better performance and more hours of sleep. With a correlation study, one does not know what causes what. Correlation does not allow for a determination of causation.

Here is another common example of incorrect conclusions from correlation research. Perhaps you have heard about studies that implicate a given part of the brain as responsible for certain types of psychopathology (e.g., ADHD). Such research has often demonstrated an association at best. Finding that certain areas of the brain show lower activity levels in children with ADHD than in control participants (those without ADHD) only shows a relationship. One cannot know for certain either that certain malfunctions in the brain are the cause of ADHD or that these malfunctions are the result of the child engaging in certain impulsive behaviors over a long period of time. Which came first? Despite the position of some people regarding the uncovering of a causal model of ADHD, only an experimental analysis can address questions of causality.

The mechanism that is lacking in correlation studies and that precludes causal analysis is the failure to actively manipulate the independent variable. Correlation studies involve only the collection of quantitative data on two sets of variables (or more variables in complex studies). No experimental manipulation takes place! Therefore, one cannot discern whether reported changes in the levels of an independent variable cause changes in the scores of the dependent variable. This inability to determine cause and effect exists irrespective of how strong the relationship is (that is, even with a high correlation coefficient). The hypothetical study described above depicting the strong correlation between sleep and test scores would have to be altered to allow for a cause-and-effect analysis. The researcher would have to systematically vary the levels of sleep in the groups of participants and assess its impact on test grades. If the level of sleep is actively manipulated, the examined relationship becomes one of cause and effect. This process of experimental manipulation will be detailed later.

Why are correlation studies not useful in applied classroom research? I stipulate several reasons. First, correlation research studies examining variables that are out of the province of the teacher are of little use to him or her. Demonstrating a relationship between parental involvement and student achievement probably will not help those teachers whose parents do not show up to parent–teacher conferences. They cannot trade in their set of parents for another set of parents, ones who are more involved with their child's education. Further, a relationship between parental involvement and student achievement, even if a strong one, does not preclude the possibility that maximizing some instructional or environmental classroom variable can override the influence of a student's home involvement in students who come from uninvolved parents. The proliferation of correlation research with variables that have little utility in classroom practice has probably contributed to practitioners' attitudes about the lack of utility of most educational research.

Correlation studies are irrelevant for practitioners for another reason. Practitioners in classrooms and schools are faced with the task of changing significant social and academic behaviors of the students they serve. Theory building is not a requisite for the classroom teacher. But getting students who are behind established grade level standards in reading to progress to grade level standards is of relevance. For teachers, research that shows a cause-and-effect relationship between an instructional method and student learning is more relevant to practice. Many people espouse the idea that contingent praise for appropriate behavior among elementary-age students is a great technique to get them to stay on task and engage in appropriate classroom behavior. Fortunately, it is more than a wishful theory. Multiple studies conducted in the 1960s and 1970s demonstrated that when the teacher was taught how to provide contingent praise for attending there was a causal effect on student behavior. The pragmatic motivation of personnel in the field would appear to depend on the utility of experimental research.

## EXPERIMENTAL RESEARCH STUDIES

### Questions to Ponder
- What is a functional relationship?
- How would you demonstrate a functional relationship between length of weekly practice time and percentage correct on tests of memorization of multiplication facts?
- Why does a researcher need to randomly assign participants to groups in group designs? What might happen if one group was markedly different on an important variable from another group in a treatment study?
- What are confounding variables?
- What is random selection? How is it different from random assignment? What does random selection allow for? What does random assignment control for?

- What are some problems with random selection of participants in applied settings?
- What are some of the limitations of group designs that you feel make them not feasible for use in school settings?

## Demonstration of a Functional Relationship

To really understand student behavior is to be able to say that A causes B, not merely that B follows A (Bailey & Bostow, 1981; Cooper et al., 2007). Demonstrating that something causes something requires that the researcher actively manipulate one variable and determine whether changes in the other variable occur. This is termed a *functional relationship* (Cooper et al., 2007). A functional relationship is demonstrated when active changes in one variable (the independent variable) produce concomitant changes in a dependent variable. Demonstrating a functional relationship between the independent variable and a dependent variable is the gold standard for discerning treatment and intervention effects. It allows you to reach conclusions on cause and effect by manipulating the independent variable and studying how such a change affects the dependent variable.

To contrast experimental research methodology with a correlation study, let's again examine the effects of sleep on test performance. The study previously referred to demonstrated a relationship between these two variables. However, we cannot conclude that getting ADHD students who have poor test scores to get more sleep would result in increased test scores. To address that question, the researcher must actively alter the level of sleep (must have at least two levels of this variable) and see if this produces differences in the test scores.

The hypothetical researcher begins her scientific inquiry by gathering a specific sample of ADHD students. To determine whether increasing sleep will affect test performance, she selects only those students with poor test grades who concurrently slept less than other ADHD students. In order to actively manipulate the amount of sleep and study, she divides this sample into two groups. The assignment of any student from the initial sample to one of the two groups is random but results in an equal number of students in each group. The study has two phases. One group (called the *control group*) receives no special instruction across both phases of the study. The members of this group continue recording the amount of sleep they get, and their teacher records their test grades at the end of the study.

The other group is the *experimental group*. For the first half of the study, the members of this group receive no special instruction, probably continuing their same pattern of sleep. But for the second phase of the study, they are given a number of strategies to get more sleep. Hence, during the second phase of the study, Group A, the control group, continues with low levels of sleep per night, whereas the members of Group B, the experimental group, after receiving the intervention procedures, increase their sleep by an average of 2.5 hours. This methodology allows for a within-group comparison of test grades across the two phases of the study for the experimental group.

However, the big question is this: Does getting more sleep produce better test grades? The members of Group B may demonstrate this if their test grades improve from the first phase of the study to the second phase of the study. Group A serves as the control, for comparison purposes. Its members' scores should not change substantially if the intervention is solely responsible for increasing test scores. One can therefore demonstrate that changing sleep duration does (or does not) affect test performance. The percentage gain across all participants in each group would answer the question empirically. Table 1.8 outlines the research process in this fictitious experimental study and presents hypothetical data on the mean percentage gain for the control and experimental groups.

The control group does not demonstrate much of a change between the two phases, I and II, in terms of test performance (see right-hand column in Table 1.8). In contrast, the experimental group shows a substantial change in mean test performance, as reflected in the right-hand column. If the difference between 4% and 25% is statistically significant, we can say that getting a student with ADHD (who is not getting enough sleep) to sleep more causes an increase in that student's test grades. As this example illustrates, cause-and-effect studies involve an active manipulation of the

Table 1.8

**RESEARCH PROCESS**

|  | PHASE I | PHASE II | MEAN % GAIN |
|---|---|---|---|
| Group A (control group) | Baseline condition | Baseline condition | 4% |
| Group B (experimental group) | Baseline condition | Treatment condition | 25% |

independent variable, also called the treatment variable. The researcher then determines whether such a change produces a change in the data obtained from measuring the dependent variable.

Here is another example demonstrating experimental manipulation of the independent variable. A teacher of American history often puts on costumes of the period she lectures about. She calls this teaching through dramatic reenactment. She has seen it on several TV shows and the students (actors) on TV all respond positively. She vehemently asserts that this is an effective technique for student learning. Does acting out periods of American history in dramatic fashion improve students' retention and comprehension of historical facts? While it may look good, does it really result in improvements in student learning? Only an experimental research study would answer that question. Such a study would determine the effects of dramatic reenactment (independent variable) on student retention and comprehension of historical facts (dependent variable).

The researcher will have to construct several tests of American history content across several weeks of lesson plans. She selects an even number of classrooms to participate in the study. In half of the classes, the teachers receive in-service training from her on using drama and costumes in their history classes. They are provided with suggestions for dramatic reenactment for each of their lesson plans. The other half of the classes do not receive any training. The comparison will be between these two groups of teachers, in terms of the students' scores on the American history tests. If the group using dramatic reenactment has history test scores that are significantly higher than those of the other group, then one can conclude that reenactment caused the change in test scores. If there is no significant difference, it did not.

Experimental research is essential to the development of an effective technology of learning and behavior change. *Too often, suggestions about effective teaching or instructional procedures are based on correlation studies.* Instructional procedures should be subjected to experimental analysis before they are counted as studies providing an evidence base for teachers. Teachers need to know that a treatment, intervention, or strategy is effective, that is, changes student behavior and/or improves student learning. Research that is only correlational in nature leaves too much of a leap of faith in terms of efficacy and does not build an evidence-based approach.

There are two forms of experimental research designs: (1) group designs (between-participant effects) and (2) single-case designs (within-subject effects). The remainder of this chapter will primarily focus on group designs, since single-case designs are the focus of the rest of the book.

## Between-Participant Effects: Group Designs

Group designs are experimental designs that determine between-participant effects. The effects of the independent variable are determined by comparing the scores of different participants on the dependent variable. The basic methodology is to randomly assign participants (from a pool of participants) to different groups. Differences between two or more treatments are determined on the basis of different test scores or student behavior. Table 1.9 provides three hypothetical examples of such studies with multiple levels of an independent variable. The independent variable can be called the treatment variable. The dependent variable will be specified as a quantitative measure of student disruptive behavior.

In the first row of Table 1.9, labeled A, the proposed study will examine the differential effectiveness of two different strategies for dealing with disruptive student behavior. A strategy termed referral to the principal for behavior problems will be compared with a time-out contingency for disruptive behavior. The level of disruptive behavior for the students in the group receiving the referral intervention will be compared with the level of disruptive behavior for the students receiving the time-out intervention.

Other comparisons can also be made. For example, in a different study, three treatments will be compared (see Table 1.9, row B). In this

Table 1.9

| THREE RESEARCH STUDIES EXAMINING VARIOUS INTERVENTIONS DEALING WITH DISRUPTIVE STUDENT BEHAVIOR | | | |
| --- | --- | --- | --- |
| ROW | RESEARCH STUDY | LEVELS OF INDEPENDENT VARIABLE | EXPERIMENTAL CONDITIONS |
| A | Study of referral vs. time out | 2 | Referral vs. time out |
| B | Study of referral vs. time out vs. ignoring | 3 | Referral vs. time out vs. ignoring |
| C | Study of referral vs. weekly counseling sessions | 2 | Referral for disruptive behavior vs. weekly counseling sessions |

proposed study, the effectiveness of referral versus time out versus ignoring the behavior will be evaluated according to the rate of disruptive behavior. Therefore, in this study, there are three levels of the treatment variable. In row C of the table, a comparison of two different referral processes, referral for disruptive behavior versus referral for counseling, will be made. The treatment variable (i.e., the independent variable) allocates the number of groups that will be needed to evaluate the number of different treatments (and controls).

Here is another study with a different dependent variable. A researcher posits that pausing after a behavior problem can be an effective strategy for handling student behavior problems. For the purposes of his research, unauthorized talking is the dependent variable. In Table 1.10, four possible studies are delineated. In the first row, two treatments are contrasted. One group will receive the pause intervention while the other will not. In row B, the researcher will have three groups. One group will receive the pause intervention. Another group will receive an intervention termed *reprimand for unauthorized talking*, while the third group will receive a response cost treatment.

In the fourth row (D), four different treatments will be compared (requiring four different groups). This study will compare different rates of pauses for each displayed target behavior. One group will get a continuous schedule of pauses, that is, 1:1, another group will get a pause every other incident of the target behavior, another group will get one pause every five target behaviors, and the final group will get no pauses (control group). This study will evaluate the efficacy of pauses as a function of schedule.

Table 1.10

**FOUR RESEARCH STUDIES**

| ROW | LEVELS OF INDEPENDENT VARIABLE | EXPERIMENTAL CONDITIONS |
|---|---|---|
| A | 2 | Pause vs. no pause |
| B | 3 | Pause vs. reprimand vs. response cost |
| C | 2 | Pause vs. behavioral contracts |
| D | 4 | Pause 1:1; pause 1:2; pause 1:5; no pause |

Suppose the researcher is interested in knowing whether the intervention is equally effective for male students as for female students. The study becomes more complicated if the effects of the actively manipulated variable are examined on an assigned variable such as gender. We then have two independent variables: treatment and gender. The results will be reported for each gender across the levels of the treatment variable (see Table 1.11). It is also possible that two studies could be conducted, one with male students (Study 1) and the other with female students (Study 2).

## Methodology of Group Designs

In using an experimental group design, several methodological requirements must be in place for the results to have a level of credibility. To have credibility, the results need to be both internally valid and externally valid. Internal validity refers to the methodology being capable of allowing the results (i.e., with regard to the dependent variable) to be attributable to the alteration of the independent variable. External validity refers to the results being generalizable to the intended population, not simply the sample.

### Random Selection and Assignment

Those selected for participation in group designs should be randomly selected from the population about which you wish to draw inferences. Random selection from a designated population allows the researcher to

Table 1.11

| EFFECTS OF PAUSING ON RATE OF UNAUTHORIZED TALKING | |
|---|---|
| **STUDY 1: MALE STUDENTS IN ELEMENTARY SCHOOL** | |
| LEVELS OF INDEPENDENT VARIABLE | EXPERIMENTAL CONDITIONS |
| 2 | Pause vs. no pause |
| **STUDY 2: FEMALE STUDENTS IN ELEMENTARY SCHOOL** | |
| LEVELS OF INDEPENDENT VARIABLE | EXPERIMENTAL CONDITIONS |
| 2 | Pause vs. no pause |

achieve a level of external validity, that is, the results of the study can be generalized to the intended population. Random selection requires that the researcher select those for participation in the study at random from among the intended population.

How does a researcher randomly select students, when all research protocols require the researcher to obtain informed consent from the parents of each child in the study? Random selection is usually not practicable in educational settings and therefore is difficult to achieve for many educational researchers. Most researchers are restricted in some manner in selecting the participant pool for a given study. They do not achieve random selection. Therefore, most experimental studies using group designs have to preface their conclusions with some discussion about the external validity[1] of the findings.

Random assignment is often easier to achieve than random selection, but it controls for a different aspect of the research methodology. In random assignment, participants are selected and then randomly assigned to the different treatment conditions. Random assignment is used to control for potential differences between the participants in each group before the study commences. You do not want differences on relevant variables between groups prior to the different treatments being implemented. For example, if you were conducting a study in which skill aptitude could have a confounding effect, randomly assigning 60 participants to one of the two treatment groups could take care of it. Just like a coin flip, about 50% of the time heads will appear and 50% of the time tails will appear. A table of random numbers is often used, or some other method of random assignment.

What can happen when a researcher does not randomly assign participants to experimental conditions? Let us say you want to determine if vitamin C results in greater strength and endurance. You devise some tests of strength and endurance. You have one group take a placebo pill (not vitamin C but looking like it). You have another group take vitamin C for 12 weeks. You find a difference between the two groups' scores on tests of strength and endurance after the 12 weeks of the experiment. You want to conclude that vitamin C is great for gaining strength and endurance.

But were the groups equal in strength and endurance prior to the study? Could the results be ascribed to a biased assignment of participants to conditions? Suppose the placebo group was culled from four sections of an introductory psychology class, and the vitamin C group was composed of physical education majors in an advanced class for bodybuilders at the same university. As you can imagine, there are probably vast initial differences between the two groups in strength and endurance prior to the experiment. The probable pretreatment differences in strength and endurance between the two groups create an ambiguous interpretation of the results of this study.

## Control for Extraneous (or Confounding) Variables

In experimental group design research, the function of the specific experimental design and method utilized is to provide a level of credibility to the conclusion. Achieving good internal validity allows the researcher to conclude that the independent variable produced changes in the dependent variable. However, alternate conclusions may be possible if the researcher did not control for possible extraneous variables or confounds. What is an extraneous or confounding variable? Think of confounding variables as alternate possible explanations of the obtained results. As an example, suppose an educational researcher assesses the math performance of students in 10 elementary school classes for a 5-week period. Her dependent variable, math performance, is measured by the students' scores on a summative math test that covers the previous 5 weeks' content. She has a theory about the students not doing well in math class. She believes that their blood is not circulating enough through the extremities, which affects the brain flow as well. Her conjecture is that some brief physical exercise prior to math period would get their blood flow going, producing more blood flow to the brain. The result should be better performance.

She initiates the study by collecting the test scores of each student for the first 5-week condition (Condition A test scores). She then provides 10 minutes of exercise for the students in all her classes before the math period for the next 5 weeks. The students take a second math test (producing Condition B test scores), this time on the content of the 5 weeks in which exercise was provided regularly. She finds that the students performed better on the second math test, that is, the test administered after the exercise condition. The average gain in test performance was 10%. She is elated that her theory has seemingly been proved accurate, and reports to the scientific community in a paper presentation that physical exercise before math results in higher math scores. Can one conclude that providing exercise causes math performance to increase? Or are there alternative explanations?

During the researcher's paper presentation, someone in the audience asks if the math period was scheduled during the morning, and if so, at what time. The teacher reports that prior to the Condition A test scores, the math period was after lunch. It remained that way for the first week of the second condition (physical activity). However, due to scheduling changes, the math period was moved to the first instructional period of the day for the remaining 4 weeks of the exercise program. A sigh goes up from the audience. Could it be that higher test scores were achieved because the second phase of the study provided math instruction in the morning, as opposed to the afternoon? As you can see, when another variable, such as time of math instruction, varies systematically with the independent variable, it creates ambiguity with respect to determining cause of change in the dependent variable.

Are there other explanations for why the test scores improved from Condition A to Condition B? Could the content have been easier during Test B? If that was the case, would a better interpretation of the change in test scores be that the change was more a function of the change in content? As you can see, a confound exists in regard to an unambiguous interpretation of the independent variable effects on the dependent variable. Alternate explanations provide a possible explanation of the changes in the test scores of the students, that is, the dependent variable. There are several types of extraneous variables that educational researchers have to control or account for when using group designs (see Table 1.12).

## Conducting a Between-Groups Design Research Study

The steps in conducting a group design cause-and-effect research study are presented in Table 1.13.

Table 1.12

**EXTRANEOUS VARIABLES**

- Could the results be a function of participant maturation?
- Could the results be accounted for by sensitization to test conditions (when pre- and posttest used, called a practice effect)?
- Could the results be ascribed to biased assignment of participants to conditions?
- Could the results be accounted for by increased loss of participants in one condition versus another (called experimental mortality)?
- Could the results be due to participant expectancy effects?

Table 1.13

STEPS TO CONDUCTING A GROUP DESIGN STUDY

- Delineate the dependent variable for the study (a variable that is relevant for student learning or behavior).

- Define the group of students who will be used in the data collection process, with the dependent variable being some measure of their behavior or skill acquisition.

- Define the independent variable (instructional approach, teacher behaviors or characteristics, school characteristics, and so forth).

- For any given independent variable, identify the treatment(s) and control condition that will be tested in your study.

- Determine which students will be assigned to which treatment or control group.

- Implement the treatment phase of the study.

- Measure the student variable in a quantitative fashion across all the students in their assigned group (the time such data is collected is determined by the actual design used).

- Subject the set of data from the dependent variable to a statistical test that determines whether the difference between the treatment group(s) and the control group is statistically significant (this is called the alpha level, usually set at .05).

## Utility of Group Designs for Classroom Teachers

While group designs provide an experimental methodology allowing a researcher to conclude that a treatment variable produces changes in the dependent variable, they are fraught with logistical problems. There are five practical limitations of group designs that make the use of such a research methodology impracticable for classroom personnel. The limitations of group designs appear to have encouraged the proliferation of single-case designs over group designs in applied settings.

The five limitations of group designs that appear to restrict their use in many applied settings and classrooms are presented in Table 1.14.

The first practical limitation of a group design is an ethical objection to the withholding of any effective treatment to participants in a control or baseline condition. A control or baseline condition involves the giving of no treatment to those groups of participants (withholding of treatment). The control group is used to evaluate an experimental treatment against possible nonspecific treatment effects and can be considered to

Table 1.14

### FIVE LIMITATIONS OF GROUP DESIGNS

- Ethicality of withholding treatment from control participant
- Impracticality of collecting a large pool of participants with same target behavior problem
- Impracticality of obtaining random samples
- Unavailability of data comparing rate of change within each participant
- Unavailability of magnitude of treatment effects for individual participants

function in a manner quite similar to the baseline condition in single-case designs. Therefore, participants assigned to the control condition in a group design do not receive treatment. In contrast, single-case designs allow for all participants to be exposed to each experimental condition and (hopefully) ultimately experience a desired change of behavior.

As an example of the first limitation of group designs, let us consider a two-group design that would experimentally examine the effect of phonics lessons on spelling tests. Such a study could be constructed in the following manner: One group would receive 20 minutes of phonics instruction. Another group would not receive such a treatment (they might receive an alternate instructional activity). As you can see, an ethical dilemma presents itself. All students in the class should be entitled to a procedure, that is, phonics, that can improve their spelling. This can be partially attended to by providing treatment after the data is collected, but some students would receive a benefit only for a shorter period of time than others.

A second limitation is the impracticability of obtaining the large number of participants necessary for group designs. If teachers are going to conduct research in their classrooms, they are hampered by the number of students in their class. If you have 20 students and want to compare four treatments, you would only have 5 students in each group. This is a small number with which to produce a statistically significant effect between one or more conditions.

A third limitation for the classroom teacher is the impracticability of obtaining random samples of participants. Group designs require random selection for the generality (generalization) of results. If this is not obtained (and it is usually difficult to obtain in an applied setting), the generality of the findings is limited. In evaluating treatments in classrooms, where the needs of individual students are of concern, it becomes unfeasible to obtain random samples for methodological purposes. Random selection is difficult for a single teacher to conduct, since the students in his or her class are not randomly selected from a target population.

A fourth limitation is the use of a single score or measure for each research participant. This does not allow for a comparison of the change that might have resulted from a change in experimental condition with any given participant. In order to individually determine how much change a given experimental condition produces, it is essential to know what the rate of the behavior was before the experimental condition was implemented, and the rate of the behavior as a result of the experimental condition. Group designs that collect only one score for each individual do not allow for a before- and after-treatment comparison for each participant.

The inability of group designs to allow for individual analyses of experimental effects (Bailey & Bostow, 1981; Cooper et al., 2007) leads to a fifth limitation. Group design methodology determines effects by averaging the scores of a number of participants. This does not allow for examination of intersubject variability of treatment effect. It is conceivable that the treatment procedure may affect some participants considerably, whereas others may be less affected (or not at all). Single-case designs, due to their measuring of the effects (behavior change) as a function of a number of different conditions, can provide data on the size of the experimental effect for each participant.

Due to these limitations, it is advisable that teachers conducting research in their own classrooms utilize single-case designs to minimize the amount of time and cost in evaluating a number of alternative treatment conditions. Group design does have a place in education research, but this methodology seems to be more appropriate for large-scale efforts to crunch achievement test data across many schools or districts.

## Introduction to Single-Case Designs

Single-case designs, like group designs, actively manipulate the treatment variable. The researcher can discern whether a given treatment produces a change in student behavior and/or learning. Single-case design is the generic term used to refer to a cause-and-effect research paradigm that has three distinctive characteristics (Bailey & Bostow, 1981; Cooper et al., 2007): (1) repeated measurements of the same behavior within a single experimental condition; (2) implementation of each treatment or experimental condition across each participant; and (3) use of the individual participant as the basis for comparison of experimental effects. In contrast to what appears to be implied by the term, single-case research designs may utilize more than one participant. You can conduct a single-case research study with many students in your class, provided the three distinctive characteristics are evidenced.

The first characteristic involves collecting data repeatedly on the same behavior (dependent variable) over a period of time. For instance, if one were to measure a student's noncompliant behavior to teacher directives in the classroom, the measurement of this child's behavior would occur repeatedly within the same condition. The child would be observed in a number of different sessions or on a number of different days, rather than being observed just once. The same behavior, noncompliance with teacher directives, is measured across time, rather than the measurement of several different behaviors being alternated. The repeated measurements within a given experimental condition can be made during multiple sessions, days, weeks, or even blocks of trials. However, each new session, day, week, or block of trials (whatever is being used) should represent another data point on a graph.

The second characteristic of a single-case design is that multiple experimental conditions (all having repeated measurements) are implemented across each participant. As was pointed out earlier, single-case designs can utilize more than one participant in the research study. Further, the study can compare different experimental conditions. However, each participant is exposed to more than one experimental condition. This allows for a comparison of any two conditions on the individual student's behavior. The determination of effectiveness is made for each individual participant.

Single-case designs measure within-participant experimental effects, in contrast to the study of between-participant effects in the case of group designs. Why is it important to assess within-participant effects? Some treatments may be effective for some students but not for others. If you average the results across an entire group, individual differences in treatment effectiveness are lost. In contrast, if each individual participant serves as the basis of comparison for each level of the independent variable, individual variation with respect to each condition will become apparent.

The remaining chapters in the book deal with single-case designs. Chapter 2 covers measurement methods for observational research, which is the primary method of measurement in single-case designs.

Chapter 3 details the characteristics of single-case designs, and it is followed by a chapter on single-case experimental designs. Chapter 5 presents information on possible categories of single-case research studies.

## NOTE

1. This is why direct replication over many studies is needed in verifying treatment efficacy.

## REFERENCES

Bailey, J. S., & Bostow, D. E. (1981). *Research methods in applied behavior analysis.* Tallahassee, FL: Copy Grafix.

Cohen, L., Manion, L., & Morrison, K. (2003). *Research methods in education* (4th ed.). New York: Taylor & Francis Routledge.

Cooper, J. O., Heron, T. F., & Heward, W. L. (2007). *Applied behavior analysis* (2nd ed.). Columbus, OH: Merrill/Prentice Hall.

Gay, L. R., Mills, G. E., & Airasian, P. (2006). *Educational research: Competencies for analysis and applications* (8th ed.). Columbus, OH: Merrill/Prentice Hall.

Gunter, P. L., Reffel, J. M., Barnett, C. A., Lee, J. M., & Patrick, J. (2004). Academic response rates in elementary-school classrooms. *Education and Treatment of Children, 27,* 105–113.

Matheson, D. W., Bruce, R. L., & Beauchamp, K. L. (1978). *Experimental psychology: Research design and analysis* (3rd ed.). Fort Worth, TX: Holt, Rinehart & Winston.

Sidman, M. (1960). *Tactics of scientific research.* New York: Basic Books.

# 2

# Measuring the Dependent Variable

Measuring the dependent variable in a quantitative fashion requires adherence to a number of methodological requirements. A direct measure of behavior is of paramount importance. To obtain reliable and valid measures of behavior and learning, a number of steps must be taken by the researcher in the construction of the observational instrument. Additionally, measures of performance may be obtained by measuring the environmental effects of a behavior. Finally, the collection of data depicting student learning is another consideration for the researcher.

## METHODOLOGICAL REQUIREMENTS FOR MEASURING STUDENT BEHAVIOR

### Questions to Ponder
- Why are direct measures preferred for applied research studies? What advantages does a direct measure of student behavior have over indirect measures? Why is inference about a phenomenon not desirable?
- In observational studies, what data should be reliable and why?

Scientific inquiry requires quantifiable measurement of the dependent variable. In applied educational research, the dependent variable is the student's behavior and/or the measure of learning. The measurement of the dependent variable in single-case designs must meet three methodological requirements. First, the measurement system used for the dependent variable must be a direct measurement of behavior. Second, it must constitute a reliable measure of student behavior and/or learning. Third, it must provide a valid measure of the phenomenon of interest.

## Direct Measurement of Behavior

A direct measurement of student behavior is the most preferred method of measurement for single-case designs. A direct measurement of behavior is the *direct observation of the behavior of interest in the setting of interest* (Hersen & Barlow, 1976). I would add to this definition the requirement for immediate recording of data, that is, *direct observation and immediate recording of the behavior of interest in the setting of interest.* A direct measure of behavior is essential to uncover cause-and-effect relationships between teacher behavior and student behavior.

Why is it necessary to obtain a direct measure? A direct measure requires minimal inference on the part of an observer to judge a phenomenon and score it as representative of a select student behavior. The less inference about what is being measured the better. The greater the level of inference, the greater the level of subjectivity and, consequently, the less reliable the data obtained.

To obtain a direct measure of student behavior, target behaviors are operationally defined in discrete, observable, quantifiable terms to allow for reliable measurement. For example, let's say you are interested in studying the variables that affect the level of disruptive behavior in children with learning disabilities. To limit your study to a specific dependent measure, you measure the occurrence of out-of-seat behavior in four identified students with learning disabilities. These students were selected because they were reported to be problematic with respect to this behavior. To observe this phenomenon, you schedule the observations to occur during math class. Out-of-seat behavior is referred to as the target behavior, and math class is referred to as the target setting. Because you are deploying a direct measure for your study, someone will directly observe the four children during math seat work and score the phenomenon as it occurs. Note that directly measuring out-of-seat behavior requires little inference on the part of the reader. The student gets out of his or her seat; the observer counts that as an instance of the behavior. The student places his or her head on the table; the observer does not count that as an occurrence of out-of-seat behavior. The scoring of the dependent measure, that is, student behavior, is fairly clear.

Suppose your research study does not want to count the number of out-of-seat instances (since that requires some effort on the part of the observer). Rather, you have the teacher estimate the rate of out-of-seat behavior on a scale from 1 to 5. While out-of-seat behavior is still the target, this rating system is an indirect measurement of the behavior problem. It requires a subjective judgment and recollection of past behavior. Asking students to fill out a survey about their out-of-seat behavior is also an indirect measure of the behavior. Whether it is a teacher's rating or the student's own rating, it introduces more inference on the part of the data collector. With more inference regarding the scoring of a phenomenon, more unreliability goes into the measurement process. Of course, the undesired effect on reliability produces an invalid measurement as well. Collecting data via checklists, projective tests, interviews, and surveys does not constitute a direct measurement of behavior. These are unacceptable proxies for measuring the problem directly. Direct measurement is achieved by observing the occurrence of a target behavior and recording that event at the time of its occurrence.

Also, measuring the behavior in a setting other than the target setting does not constitute a direct measurement of behavior. Why insist on measuring the phenomenon of interest in the setting(s) of interest? One should not assume that the level of any given behavior is constant across a variety of different contexts and conditions. Here are some examples. If we are interested in determining what the level of aggression is for five students on the playground, should we observe them during music class? You can see that it is quite plausible that these students may be more aggressive on the playground than during music class. Therefore, collecting data on the aggression levels during music class may not be a valid measure of their aggression on the playground.

## Reliable and Valid Measurement

Reliability is a term you often hear. For example, an advertisement on TV poses the following question: How reliable is your underarm deodorant in keeping you dry, even in stressful situations? In this example, reliability refers to consistency. Will the deodorant keep your underarms dry time after time? If it works one time but not another, it is not consistent in its effect; hence it is unreliable.

What do we mean when we say that the research data on the dependent variable are reliable? How do we demonstrate that? Here is a concrete example. Let us say I want to measure how many red geometric shapes can be found in a preschool classroom. If I show two people the same geometric shape, unreliable data would be obtained if one person says he or she saw a reddish square and the other says he or she saw a green square. If they both report the color of that square as purple, or they both report seeing red as the color, we have agreement between these two observers, and hence reliability. If they consistently agree on the color of a number of geometric shapes, we would say that their reports of the color of various objects are reliable (across observers).

We determine accuracy by determining the degree to which the same data set is recorded by independent observers. If two people watch the same phenomenon, their reports of the phenomenon should not be so discrepant that it seems as if they were watching completely different events. Let's look at an example that illustrates this point.

You can have a reliable measurement instrument but not have a valid measure of the phenomenon. Using a direct measurement of the phenomenon of interest is essential for obtaining a valid measure of student behavior. If an indirect measure is used, greater inference is required, and additional steps are often needed to establish the validity of the measurement.

## STEPS TO MEASURING STUDENT BEHAVIOR

### Questions to Ponder

- What do you think is the effect of inadequate behavioral descriptions of the dependent variable on observer agreement?
- What are some classroom or school circumstances in which you would want to collect a continuous measure, and when would time sampling be more appropriate?
- Why do you think it is necessary to train observers in a research study?
- Are there some practical advantages of collecting frequency data in contrast to duration measures?
- What behaviors are best measured with a duration measure?

- How are latency data different from cumulative duration data?
- What is the relationship between reliability and validity? Can you have one without the other?

The steps presented in Table 2.1 detail the process of directly observing student behavior.

## Developing and Utilizing Behavioral Descriptions

The initial task in developing an observational instrument for the classroom is to develop a behavioral description of the variable. The behavioral description provides an operational definition of the phenomenon, delineating specific, observable behaviors. It requires little inference on the part of the observer. Observable behaviors such as sitting, standing, crawling, walking, running, hitting, spitting, kicking, getting out of a seat, breaking class rules (if defined in some manner), and completing seat work require minimal inference on the part of the observer engaged in viewing the student's behavior. Unobservable traits, such as being understanding, respectful, incorrigible, psychotic, ill mannered, or appreciative or showing awareness, do not allow for an accurate objective measurement unless defined in observable terms.

Specifying observable behaviors allows for a more accurate measurement of student behavior. For example, one can see a child hit someone, or a child not comply with a teacher's request. These behaviors are observable and allow the teacher to determine how often they occur, by counting the number of times a specific child hits another child (or the number of times specific children hit other children). In contrast, one

Table 2.1

### SIX STEPS TO COLLECTING OBSERVATIONAL DATA

1. Developing and utilizing behavioral descriptions
2. Determining when data will be collected, that is, the observation session
3. Determining the observational measurement method
4. Determining the reliability of observational data
5. Training observers
6. Collecting permanent product data

cannot see a child's hyperactivity. *Hyperactivity* is a term that describes a constellation of behaviors. It would be very hard to measure hyperactivity in an objective manner because everyone has a different interpretation of what constitutes hyperactivity. While such a diagnostic label may have its place in the medical field, it is not useful as a primary dependent variable in research that requires a direct measurement of behavior.

What happens if you attempt to conduct direct measurement of vague, unobservable entities instead of a pinpointed target problem behavior? Ambiguous descriptions, such as lazy, disturbed, or impulsive, lead to unreliability in the observer's recording of the frequency of behavior. Just imagine if someone asked you to make a tally mark every time you saw a student being lazy in the classroom. Would you have trouble scoring such a phenomenon? You bet! Your judgment of laziness would certainly change from one day to the next. Further, your judgment and another person's judgment of laziness could be fairly discrepant (and therefore unreliable). How can any other information that is tied to such data collection be accurate? It cannot!

Defining the target behavior can be difficult. There are two major methods you can utilize to generate behavioral descriptions from ambiguous entities. An effective method to help you develop behavioral descriptions of the dependent variable is to schedule time yourself to observe the phenomenon in the intended classroom(s). This will allow you to view the phenomenon of interest and develop a behavioral description. Select a time when it is highly likely that the behavior of interest will occur. Then you can formulate a behavioral description that matches what you observed.

Another method is to search the research literature for definitions used in studies that have measured the dependent variable you are interested in. Table 2.2 provides you with a listing of studies and the operational definitions used to measure the dependent variable. In Table 2.2, the dependent variable is underlined and the behavioral description used in the study is given below it in the right hand column.

## Determining When Data Will Be Collected

The next step is to determine when the data will be collected and for how long. This is referred to as the observation schedule. The observation schedule delineates the length and number of observation sessions for the research study. An observation session is defined by the times at which an observation is initiated and terminated. Research studies

Table 2.2

## DEFINITIONS OF COMMON CLASSROOM PROBLEM BEHAVIORS

| REFERENCE | BEHAVIOR/DEFINITION |
|---|---|
| Hall, Lund, & Jackson, 1968 | <u>study behavior</u><br>orientation toward appropriate person or object |
| Thomas, Becker, & Armstrong, 1968 | <u>disruptive behavior</u><br>*gross motor*<br>getting out of seat, running, hopping, rocking, moving chair<br>*noise making*<br>tapping feet, clapping, rattling, slamming or tapping objects on desk<br>*orienting*<br>turning head and/or body away from teacher<br>*verbalization*<br>conversing with other students, calling out the teacher's name, coughing loudly<br>*aggression*<br>obviously hitting any part of self or another person |
| Zeilberger, Sampen, & Sloane, 1968 | <u>bossing</u><br>directing another child or adult to do (or not do) something |
| Madsen, Becker, & Thomas, 1968 | <u>inappropriate classroom behavior</u><br>three areas: *gross motor* (running, etc.), *object noise* (tapping pencil, etc.), and *disturbance of others' property* (grabbing objects)<br><u>appropriate behavior</u><br><u>time on task</u> |
| Phillips, 1968 | <u>aggressive statements</u><br>stated or threatened inappropriate destruction of or damage to object, person, or animal (e.g., "If you don't shut up, I'm going to kill you")<br><u>punctuality</u><br>three contexts: (1) *returning from school,* (2) *going to bed,* and (3) *returning from errand*<br><u>poor grammar</u><br>"ain't" |
| Walker & Buckley, 1968 | <u>attending behavior (on task)</u><br>looking at assignment pages, working problems, recording responses |

*(continued)*

Table 2.2

## DEFINITIONS OF COMMON CLASSROOM PROBLEM BEHAVIORS (*CONTINUED*)

| REFERENCE | BEHAVIOR/DEFINITION |
|---|---|
| | nonattending behavior<br>    those incompatible with above |
| Ward & Baker,<br>1968 | disruptive behaviors<br>*motor behavior (at seat)*<br>*gross motor behavior (not at seat)*<br>*aggression*<br>*deviant talking*<br>*nonattending disobedience*<br>*thumb sucking*<br>*hand raising* |
| O'Leary, Becker, Evans,<br>& Saudargas, 1969 | disturbing another's property<br>    tearing up others' paper, grabbing their book(s)<br>inappropriate tasks<br>    working on spelling during math, doodling |
| Zimmerman, Zimmerman,<br>& Russell, 1969 | instruction-following behaviors<br>    30 instructions |
| Barrish, Saunders, &<br>Wolf, 1969 | talking out, out of seat |
| Wahler, 1969 | oppositional behavior<br>    failure to follow request of parent |
| Schmidt & Ulrich,<br>1969 | classroom noise<br>    sound-level meter 42 db or higher |
| Cantrell, Cantrell,<br>Huddleston, &<br>Woolridge, 1969 | assignment completion |
| Schutte & Hopkins,<br>1970 | instruction following (kindergarten)<br>    10 common instructions |
| Bailey, Phillips, &<br>Wolf, 1970 | violations of following six rules<br>    (1) do not leave seat without permission, (2) do<br>    not talk without permission, (3) do not look out<br>    the window, (4) do not tilt desks, (5) do not<br>    make noise, and (6) do not disturb others |

*Note.* Taken from *Functional Behavioral Assessment, Diagnosis, and Treatment: A Complete System for Education and Mental Health Settings,* by E. Cipani and K. Schock, 2007. New York: Springer Publishing. Reprinted with permission.

are composed of many observation sessions. It is important to make a decision early in the research process on how the data will be collected: continuously or via time samplings.

A continuous measure in school settings is obtained when the observer detects every instance of the behavior (Cooper, Heron, & Heward, 2007). For example, you might be interested in studying the instruction-following behavior of children in elementary grade class-rooms. A continuous measure of instruction-following behavior across the entire school day may be necessary. The teacher or researcher will observe the child for the entire school day and note each occurrence of instruction-following behavior. In some cases, you may decide that a continuous measure of the targeted behavior(s) needs to be collected.

One of the disadvantages of a continuous measure of behavior is time commitment. You may not have the entire day, every day, to watch students so that you can collect your research data. Further, it might not be feasible for on-site personnel to perform a continuous measure in ad-dition to their other duties. In these circumstances, you might consider a time sampling data collection method for these personnel to use. Time sampling involves observing and measuring the behavior of interest in a select number of time periods within an observation schedule.

Let's say you are interested in studying disruptive behavior and how certain interventions influence the rate of such behavior. You select three classes in which to conduct your study. Are you going to observe all day in each classroom? Rather than resorting to a continuous measure, you de-vise an observation schedule that samples each of these classrooms daily. You schedule observations for three 15-minute time periods for each classroom during the 6-hour school day. You continue this observation schedule across a 1- or 2-week period. Table 2.3 gives the start times for each of three observation periods for these classrooms for a given day.

Table 2.3

### OBSERVATION SCHEDULE ACROSS THREE CLASSROOMS

| OBSERVATION PERIOD | CLASSROOM A | CLASSROOM B | CLASSROOM C |
|---|---|---|---|
| 1 | 9:00 | 9:45 | 10:00 |
| 2 | 11:00 | 11:30 | 10:45 |
| 3 | 1:30 | 1:10 | 2:00 |

The specific observations scheduled across each classroom should be representative of the entire school day. Therefore it is wise to alternate the observation schedule regularly (perhaps daily) for each classroom. Thus, Classroom A (or Classrooms B and C) would not be observed at the same time every day. In this manner, the sample of behavior obtained across many days becomes representative of the times when no observation takes place.

It is helpful to provide the observer(s) at the sites with the tools to use in collecting observational data. Below is a list of possible tools that facilitate the collection of data (Bailey & Bostow, 1981):

1. Wrist counters (for frequency measures)
2. Data sheets delineating behavior(s) to observe
3. Stopwatches (for duration measures)
4. Tape recorders (for interval recording measures)

## Determining the Observational Measurement Method

Once the behavioral description is complete, the researcher can then designate the method for measuring and quantifying the level of behavior. Quantifying a behavior refers to the way in which the target behavior will be scored or counted. There are three main methods of measuring an observable behavior: (1) frequency, (2) duration, and (3) interval recording.

*Frequency* measurement or event recording (Cooper et al., 2007) involves counting the number of occurrences of a target behavior (Bailey & Bostow, 1981; Hersen & Barlow, 1976). Every time the behavior occurs, regardless of the length of time for which it occurs, it is counted. Frequency counts are well suited for behaviors that have distinctive beginnings and endings. For example, the frequency of eye contact in children with autism and mental retardation was measured as to its occurrence after the verbal prompt "Look at me!" was given (Foxx, 1977). A rate of occurrence was developed for each session, which showed variability across the sessions.

Teachers who are interested in getting children to complete more class assignments could use a frequency measure (Robinson, Newby, & Ganzell, 1981). Such researchers may count the number of completed assignments for each child each day across different assignments. A convenient and easy-to-use data sheet for one student is presented in Table 2.4. It provides a space for counting the number of assignments completed (see second column). The user then records how many assignments were completed over the total number of assignments required that day (see third column). The hypothetical data for one student presented in Table 2.4 shows that on March 3, four assignments were completed out of five total assignments for that day. The data for the remaining three days depict the number of assignments completed and the total ratio.

A frequency count could be used to measure out-of-seat behavior. Fortunately, out-of-seat behavior has a distinct beginning and end. The behavior begins with the student's body losing physical contact with the chair and ends when the student's body contacts the chair and/or desk again. This constitutes one occurrence of out-of-seat behavior. The data sheet in Table 2.5 illustrates a frequency measure of out-of-seat behavior from June 1 through June 8 (6 school days). For each date,

Table 2.4

**DATA SHEET FOR MEASURING ASSIGNMENT COMPLETION FOR ONE STUDENT**

| DATE | ASSIGNMENTS COMPLETED | ASSIGNMENT COMPLETION RATIO |
|------|------------------------|------------------------------|
| March 3 | 4 | 4:5 |
| March 4 | 2 | 2:5 |
| March 5 | 5 | 5:6 |
| March 6 | 5 | 5:5 |

Table 2.5

**FREQUENCY DATA SHEET FOR OUT-OF-SEAT BEHAVIOR**

| DATE | | | | | FREQUENCY | | | | | | | |
|------|---|---|---|---|---|---|---|---|---|----|----|----|----|
| June 1 | 1 | 2 | 3 | 4 | 5 | 6 | | | | | | | |
| June 2 | 1 | 2 | 3 | 4 | 5 | 6 | 7 | | | | | | |
| June 3 | 1 | 2 | 3 | 4 | 5 | 6 | 7 | 8 | 9 | 10 | 11 | | |
| June 4 | 1 | 2 | 3 | 4 | 5 | 6 | 7 | 8 | | | | | |
| June 5 | 1 | 2 | 3 | 4 | 5 | 6 | 7 | 8 | 9 | 10 | 11 | 12 | 13 |
| June 8 | 1 | 2 | 3 | 4 | 5 | 6 | 7 | 8 | 9 | 10 | 11 | 12 | 13 |

the user writes the number of the incident in the appropriate box. Therefore the frequency of each occurrence is recorded as the highest number written. For example, on June 1, there are six occurrences of out-of-seat behavior, and on June 2 there are seven.

*Duration* data collection involves determining the cumulative length of time for which a behavior occurs. The length of time for which a behavior occurs can be an important measure. Some behaviors may occur infrequently, yet the duration of each episode is extremely lengthy. Suppose I tell you that a child has about one tantrum every couple of days and is 4 years old. You might wonder why anyone would complain about that! Many 4-year-olds have multiple tantrums daily. Now I tell you that this child's tantrum lasts 30–50 minutes. Therefore, simply providing a frequency count of this child's tantrums gives an inaccurate picture of the problem. In these circumstances, a duration measure would be preferred over a frequency count. Table 2.6 provides a sample data sheet measuring the duration of verbal disruption for a hypothetical student.

The data sheet presents 2 days' worth of data on duration of tantrum behavior for each episode. On April 22, the student had three tantrums: the first one lasted 2 minutes and 25 seconds; the second lasted 3 minutes and 44 seconds; and the third lasted all of 10 minutes and 55 seconds. The cumulative duration of tantrum behavior for that day was 17 minutes and 4 seconds.

*Response latency* is also a duration measure, but it quantifies a different aspect of behavior. Latency measures quantify how quickly a behavior occurs after some designated starting point. For example, recording the amount of time that elapses before a student complies with a given teacher request would constitute a response latency measure. In this

## Table 2.6

**SAMPLE DATA SHEET DURATION**

| DISRUPTIVE INCIDENT DATE | FIRST | SECOND | THIRD | FOURTH | FIFTH | TOTAL DURATION |
|---|---|---|---|---|---|---|
| April 22 | 2'25" | 3'44" | 10'55" | | | 17'4" |
| April 23 | 55' | 21'14" | | | | 22'9" |
| April 24 | | | | | | |
| April 25 | | | | | | |

example, response latency may be more important than frequency of compliance. Suppose the researcher collects the frequency of a student's compliance to teacher instructions. The resulting data show a high rate of compliance. Should we conclude that everything is tolerable with respect to compliance? Not necessarily. When we collect data on the latency of compliance to the teacher instruction, the data reveal a significant problem. The latency data reveal that this student initiates compliance about 2–4 minutes subsequent to the teacher request. One cannot be happy with a student who waits that long to comply. Latency of response is the criterion measure in this hypothetical study, because the student's slow compliant response is the crux of the compliance problem.

*Interval recording* measures involve dividing an observation session into a number of continuous, equally timed intervals. Interval lengths are commonly 5, 10, or 15 seconds. Therefore, in a 30-minute observation session, there will be 360 intervals if you are using a 5-second interval recording method, 180 intervals if the interval length is 10 seconds, and 120 intervals if the interval length is 15 seconds.

The data yielded from an interval recording system are percentages of occurrence. The researcher counts the number of intervals for which the target behavior is scored and divides that number by the total number of intervals. For example, in an interval recording system that has 6 intervals per minute and 20 minutes for a given observation session, there will be 120 total intervals. If the target behavior is recorded in 12 intervals in the first observation session, the ratio is 12:120 or 10% occurrence for that session.

There are two methods for scoring behavior in an interval recording system (Powell, Martindale, & Kulp, 1975): (1) the whole interval method and (2) the partial interval method. The whole interval method scores the occurrence of the behavior if the behavior occurs for the entire length of the interval. Therefore, with intervals of 10 seconds, the child must exhibit the behavior for the entire 10-second interval in order for it to be scored as occurring. If it occurs for less than 10 seconds, then it will not be scored. If a behavior begins in one interval and ends in another, it may not be scored in either interval unless it occurs across the first and/or second interval.

The partial interval method scores the occurrence of the behavior if the behavior occurs for any part of the interval. Therefore, if the child exhibits the behavior for only 2 of the 10 seconds of the interval, it will be scored as occurring in that interval. In a partial interval scoring system, the user records the occurrence of the behavior if any instance occurs within a given interval, no matter how short its duration. It is often possible for a behavior to start in one interval and end in another interval. Both intervals will be scored.

With intervals of longer lengths (e.g., 30 seconds, 1 minute), the whole interval method will provide an underestimate of the level of behavior (Powell et al., 1975). In the partial interval method, with intervals over 30 seconds, an overestimate will occur (Powell, Martindale, Kulp, Martindale, & Bowman, 1977). The larger the interval, the greater the discrepancy between these two methods of scoring (whole and partial interval), and the *true duration of behavior*. For example, interval lengths of 5 minutes yield data that will be very discrepant from a continuous duration measure in the same time period. Suffice it to say, intervals of 5 or 10 seconds minimize such a discrepancy and are advocated when utilizing an interval recording system.

There are several different methods of observing and recording behaviors using an interval recording system (Smith, Madsen, & Cipani, 1981). One method is termed the *continuous method*, which involves watching and scoring the behaviors simultaneously in each interval (described above). A second method is termed the *observe and record system*. In this system, the observer merely watches the behavior in one interval and records the occurrence of the behavior in the following interval. This means that he or she observes and then records. This system separates the function of observing and recording. A third method is termed the *5/10 method*. In this method, the observer watches and scores for the first five intervals (of a 10-second interval recording system) and then rests on the sixth interval. The last-mentioned two methods were designed on the assumption that having observers perform fewer functions in each interval would produce more reliable data. However, empirical data do not support that contention (Smith et al., 1981).

Another form of interval recording involves observing at the end of a given interval and determining whether the behavior occurred during that brief observation. It is often referred to as *momentary time sampling* and is well suited for data collection by existing personnel. For example, if a researcher designates 5-minute intervals for a 2-hour observation session, she can designate the last 10 seconds as the time sampling period. Therefore, for the first 4 minutes and 50 seconds of each 5-minute interval, the researcher can engage in other instructional activities. For the last 10 seconds, marked by a sound audible to the researcher only, he or she watches the student(s) to determine whether the target behavior occurs or not. If it occurs in that time period, it is recorded. This momentary time sampling observation system merely requires direct observation for

10 seconds in each 5-minute interval. Momentary time sampling has been shown to more accurately estimate a continuous duration measure than the partial or whole interval recording methods (Harop & Daniels, 1986; Powell et al., 1977). Momentary time sampling recording systems are well suited for use by the teacher.

One application of momentary time sampling in educational settings is the beeper system (Cipani, 2008). The beeper system monitors the on-task behavior of a student, a group of students, or an entire class in a momentary time sampling method. It is well suited for teachers in that it allows them to collect data while still being able to deliver instruction to the class. At variable intervals, a vibrating stimulus or beep sounds (inaudible to the class but audible to the teacher). At that point in time, the teacher views the target students or groups of students. She judges whether they are displaying on-task behavior or not at that time only. Points are awarded for on-task behavior that is observed at that time. The same process is deployed at each beep, at which a momentary sample of on-task behavior is taken and scored. By using this form of momentary time sampling procedure, the teacher can return to her instructional activities after engaging in the brief data collection effort. In this regard, momentary time sampling is preferable to a continuous measure of on-task behavior.

## Determining the Reliability of Observational Data

In traditional measurement, because one score is used as a representation of what would be obtained under similar conditions in another testing, the reliability of the obtained score must be high across different items (that measure the same skill), different times (test–retest), and of course scoring (consistency across different test graders). With observational data, the requirement, when using single-case designs, to collect samples of behavior repeatedly across time obviates the need to determine if one score is an accurate measure across time. Situational variability, to a great extent, is captured rather than statistically controlled. The requirement for reliability in single-case research designs involves the degree to which the observers (the measurement instrument) concur that the defined behavior did or did not occur. Hence, the degree of interobserver agreement is the primary requisite and index for determining the reliability of observational data in single-case designs.

In most applied research studies, reliability checks are deployed to ascertain the level of interobserver agreement. Such a check involves two people independently observing and recording the same phenomenon at the same time. If one student is being observed, then both the primary observer and the reliability observer watch this student for the entire observation period. If several students are being observed, or the entire class, both observers use the same recording sheet and observational process to collect data.[1] They then compare their results for concordance. The actual formulas for computing this across frequency, duration, and interval data are presented in appendix A.

In a reliability check, one observer is usually termed the primary observer. This person is the one who collects data frequently, for example, the teacher, the researcher, or someone who is assigned specifically to data collection. The reliability observer is the person who usually just conducts the reliability checks. The scores are compared in the manner designated in appendix A. Reliability checks should generally constitute at least 20% of the total number of observation sessions. Additionally, there should be a proportional number of reliability checks for each condition. One would not conduct 10 reliability checks in one condition versus only one reliability check in another experimental condition.

## Observer Training

Observers are trained to immediately score the occurrence of the behavior(s) according to a prespecified set of criteria (Cipani & McLaughlin, 1981). If you are conducting a research study, it is important to treat the development of accurate observational skills using the recording form as a skill requiring time and effort. This is a requisite even if you will use only one primary observer. A reliability observer must also be used in a research study, and hence efforts to ensure that the two observers will agree frequently on the occurrence or nonoccurrence of behavior is essential. Observer training should incorporate the following: (1) discrimination between examples of the target behavior and those phenomena that do not constitute the target behavior, (2) use of a specific recording form and any additional apparatus required, and (3) ability to summate scores over a given session and record such data in the designated place.

First, observers should be taught the operational definition(s) of the behavior(s) you intend to observe. For research studies, a formal observer training phase should be incorporated into your written plan and reported in your write-up. You should provide a written manual when appropriate for the observers to read. You should describe examples of the target behavior as well as examples of behaviors they might observe that are not scored as the target behavior.

Observer training can also involve the potential observers watching videotape sequences and scoring the targeted behaviors using the form you have designed. Observers' scores are compared to a scoring you have developed by repeatedly watching these tape segments and scoring the target behaviors. This is called a *criterion scoring*. The criterion scoring is used to compare the observers' scoring of a particular segment of videotape with a scoring obtained over repeated observations by you. This will allow for a comparison with a segment that is highly accurate (i.e., criterion scoring). Finally, you should teach the observers how to tabulate the session data to a criterion of 100% accuracy. You of course will also tabulate such data to make it more reliable.

Finally, in collecting observational data, there are some additional requirements. These are depicted in Table 2.7.

## Collecting Permanent Product Data

### Questions to Ponder

- How can permanent product data be valuable in ascertaining the experimental effect? What information may such data give you that observational data on student behavior may not provide?
- What are some of the situations in which you would collect permanent product data and what would such data be?
- Why would norm-referenced tests be impractical in single-case designs? What happens with repeated administration of norm-referenced tests?

Table 2.7

**ADDITIONAL REQUIREMENTS FOR COLLECTING OBSERVATIONAL DATA**

- Standardize the observation schedule: Set schedules for the observations with the observers who will collect data.
- Schedule observers' training times.
- Schedule observers and reliability checks.
- Schedule regular collection of data forms: Pick up data forms from the research site regularly to prevent losing data.

Sometimes data can be collected on human performance without the behavior itself being observed. Rather, the product, or the enduring physical evidence that such a behavior did in fact occur, can be measured (Bailey & Bostow, 1981). Obviously, the effect on the physical environment must last long enough to allow for retrieval by humans. Permanent product measurement involves specifying the environmental conditions that will result if the behavior is performed at some criterion level (Cooper et al., 2007). Anything that ends up on a piece of paper or makes an electronic imprint allows for a measurement of that product.

Suppose you are interested in measuring the level of on-task behavior during independent reading that is part of a language arts period of 25 minutes. You consider collecting observational data on all 24 students in the class. If an interval recording system is going to be used, it will require at least two observers to become adept at using the system. A permanent product measure might be well suited to this situation. Perhaps a paper assignment can be used as a permanent product measure. When students turn in their assignment, their performance on the assignment leaves a permanent record of the behavior. If the students were consistently on task, one would hypothesize that their assignments would often be complete. Therefore, a researcher might just measure the accuracy of the completed assignments as the dependent variable for a study. There are several advantages in using permanent product data in a research study (see Table 2.8).

Some research studies have used permanent product data to supplement observational data. In one study, the rate of food spillage

## Table 2.8

### ADVANTAGES OF COLLECTING PERMANENT PRODUCT DATA

- Allows freedom to engage in instructional activities
- Can measure behavior that occurs at times when it would be inconvenient to observe
- May be more accurate than observational data
- Use of audio or video tapes facilitates data collection efforts and recording of data.

*Note.* Taken from *Functional Behavioral Assessment, Diagnosis, and Treatment: A Complete System for Education and Mental Health Settings,* by E. Cipani and K. Schock, 2007. New York: Springer Publishing. Reprinted with permission.

during mealtimes of an institutionalized resident with mental retardation was the target behavior (Cipani, 1981). Across various treatment conditions, the author counted the number of spillages per meal directly. At the point where the program had to be implemented by direct care staff in the unit cafeteria, another method of data collection was employed. The aides measured the result of the client's mealtime behavior according to the amount of food spillage evidenced upon completion of the meal. The procedure required that the aides be notified by the resident that she had finished her meal. The aides would then count the number of spots of food spillage on the table, on her person, and in the general vicinity. If less than three spots of spillage were evident, she earned points to be traded in later. Other examples of behaviors that might be measured through permanent product data could be dressing skills, furniture cleaning, compliance with certain tasks involving a finished product, homework, and any other behaviors resulting in a paper-and-pencil task (see criterion-referenced tests, discussed below).

There are two disadvantages of using permanent product measures. The first problem occurs when other behaviors have some influence on the permanent product measure. In order to ensure an accurate, reliable estimate of observable behavior without direct observation, the product should be a function only of the target behavior being measured. A related second problem area is the ability of the permanent product data to provide distinctions in performance of the target behavior. For example, one occurrence of the behavior should produce a lasting output that is markedly different than the output that would have been derived from or produced by 10 occurrences.

## MEASURING STUDENT LEARNING

Student learning is measured in a quantitative fashion via tests. The tests can be either norm referenced or criterion referenced. Norm-referenced tests are usually commercially available. They allow for a comparison of students' scores on the test to a group norm, for example, in chronological age or grade level comparisons. Grade or age equivalents delineate where a given student's score resides with regard to the scores of same-age peers on this test. While such tests are good for demonstrating summary progress over a lengthy intervention, their use on a more frequent basis in repeated measurement designs is not practicable. Therefore, the discussion of measuring student learning will focus on the utilization of criterion-referenced tests or measurements.

What is a *criterion-referenced test*? A criterion-referenced test measures very specific skills (see Table 2.9). Test items are designed on the basis of the skill being assessed. Test results are analyzed relative to the skill being assessed. Students' performance on such tests is interpreted from the standpoint of their performance with respect to the mastery level of performance designated for that skill. The mastery level of performance is established through the specification of a criterion level of performance for the skill(s). Mastery levels specify the objective criteria defining competence for each specific skill. Due to the fact that criterion-referenced assessment is objective or performance referenced, the data obtained readily identify each student's deficiencies in skills and the skills acquired by each student.

How are criterion-referenced tests used in research studies? If you are interested in collecting data on learning in a particular classroom, you must have a dependent measure that will be sensitive to what is being taught. It does not make sense to evaluate the efficacy of an instructional method with regard to skills that were not included in the content area. For example, if you are determining the effectiveness of a teach-and-test method of spelling words, you will not use a test of algebra to evaluate how well the instructional approach worked! Rather, you would design several spelling tests using the targeted words and present several different but parallel tests to measure student learning.

Here is an excellent illustration of a research study that utilized criterion-referenced tests as a primary dependent variable. In a study

Table 2.9

**CRITERION-REFERENCED TESTS**

- Measure specific skills and are constructed to measure just the designated skill
- Are derived from an instructional objective that has three components
- Allow for a comparison between the students' performance on the skill and a criterion level of competence
- Allow for a direct relationship between assessment and the instructional needs of the child
- Do not contrast scores of one student with those of other students
- Do not require normative standardized data for a representative sample group

that examined hand raising versus response cards with regard to acquisition of learning in a fourth-grade class, the researchers constructed 10-item tests for each lesson presentation (Narayan, Heward, Gardner, Courson, & Omness, 1990). The results are presented in Figure 2.1.

Many criterion-referenced assessments are teacher designed. This means that the teacher identifies the skill(s), designs items that directly measure the skill(s), and then presents these to the students. First, you must identify the instructional objective. Skills need to be translated into performance or instructional objectives (Dick & Carey, 1985; Mager, 1975). These objectives should be composed of three essential components (Mager, 1975): (1) the observable measurable behavior, (2) the criterion level of performance, and (3) the conditions of assessment.

The specific behavior must be delineated. For example, there is an instructional objective that specifies an observable behavior: "the student will add three 3-digit numbers with carry to 10s and 100s place." It is very clear that the teacher would see if this student performs the desired behavior. In contrast, "the student will know the place value of problems with carry" does not specify an observable entity. What behavior would one see when a student "knows" something? The criterion level of performance is specified to indicate when a student is competent in the skill contained in the given objective. Specifying 80% correct responses indicates the point that separates those who have achieved mastery and those who require more instruction. Finally, the conditions of the assessment, such as a paper-and-pencil or oral test, together with other items,

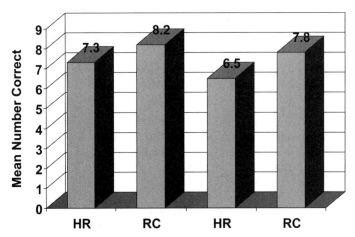

**Figure 2.1** Hand raising (HR) versus response cards (RC) on daily test grades: results on 10-item tests.

such as whether the test is timed or not, provide the relevant conditions under which the student's behavior will be examined. The form of the test items then has to be determined, that is, whether the items should be in multiple choice, true-false, short answer, or other exam formats.

## SUMMARY

Measuring the dependent variable in observational research studies requires one to attend to three methodological requirements. First, a direct measure of the phenomenon is greatly preferred, if not essential. Second, measurement of the dependent variable must be reliable, requiring that different observers report with high concordance the incidence of the phenomenon of interest. Finally, the direct measure must be a valid measure of the phenomenon of interest. Given those considerations, there are six steps to collecting observational data. They are as follows: (1) developing and utilizing behavioral descriptions; (2) determining when data will be collected, that is, the observation session; (3) determining the observational measurement method; (4) determining the reliability of observational data; (5) training observers; and (6) collecting permanent product data. Measures of student learning often involve criterion-referenced tests, designed by the teacher. It is crucial that such testing occur repeatedly throughout each condition.

### NOTE

1. Reliability checks would not involve one observer watching one student while the other is watching another, and then comparing their results.

### REFERENCES

Bailey, J. S., & Bostow, D. E. (1981). *Research methods in applied behavior analysis.* Tallahassee, FL: Copy Grafix.

Bailey, J. S., Phillips, E. L., & Wolf, M. M. (1970). Home-based reinforcement and the modification of pre-delinquents' classroom behavior. *Journal of Applied Behavior Analysis, 3,* 223–233.

Barrish, H. H., Saunders, M., & Wolf, M. M. (1969). Good Behavior Game: Effects of individual contingencies for group consequences on disruptive behavior in a classroom. *Journal of Applied Behavior Analysis, 2,* 119–124.

Cantrell, R. P., Cantrell, M. L., Huddleston, C. M., & Woolridge, R. L. (1969). Contingency contracting with school problems. *Journal of Applied Behavior Analysis, 2,* 215–220.

Cipani, E. (1981). Modifying food spillage in an institutionalized retarded client. *Journal of Behavior Therapy and Experimental Psychiatry, 12,* 261–265.

Cipani, E. (2008). *Classroom management for all teachers: Evidence-based plans.* Columbus, OH: Merrill/Prentice Hall.

Cipani, E., & McLaughlin, T. F. (1981). A procedural analysis for conducting observer training for observational research. *Corrective and Social Psychiatry, 27,* 125–129.

Cipani, E., & Schock, K. (2007). *Functional behavioral assessment, diagnosis, and treatment: A complete system for education and mental health settings.* New York: Springer Publishing.

Cooper, J. O., Heron, T. F., & Heward, W. L. (2007). *Applied behavior analysis* (2nd ed.). Columbus, OH: Merrill/Prentice Hall.

Dick, W., & Carey, L. (1985). *The systematic design of instruction* (2nd ed.). Glencoe, IL: Scott Foresman.

Foxx, R. M. (1977). Attention training: The use of overcorrection to increase the eye contact of autistic and retarded children. *Journal of Applied Behavior Analysis, 10,* 489–499.

Hall, R. V., Lund, D., & Jackson, D. (1968). Effects of teacher attention on study behavior. *Journal of Applied Behavior Analysis, 1,* 1–12.

Harop, A., & Daniels, M. (1986). Methods of time sampling: A reappraisal of momentary time sampling and partial interval recording. *Journal of Applied Behavior Analysis, 19,* 73–77.

Hart, B. M., Reynolds, N. J., Baer, D. M., Brawley, E. R., & Harris, F. R. (1968). Effect of contingent and non-contingent social reinforcement on the cooperative play of a preschool child. *Journal of Applied Behavior Analysis, 1,* 73–76.

Hersen, M., & Barlow, D. H. (1976). *Single-case experimental designs: Strategies in studying behavior change.* New York: Pergamon Press.

Madsen, C. H., Jr., Becker, W. C., & Thomas, D. R. (1968). Rules, praise, and ignoring: Elements of elementary classroom control. *Journal of Applied Behavior Analysis, 1,* 139–150.

Mager, R. F. (1975). *Preparing instructional objectives.* Belmont, CA.: Fearon.

Narayan, J. S., Heward, W. L., Gardner, R., Courson, F. H., & Omness, C. K. (1990). Using response cards to increase student participants in an elementary classroom. *Journal of Applied Behavior Analysis, 23,* 483–490.

O'Leary, K. D., Becker, W. C., Evans, M. B., & Saudargas, R. A. (1969). A token reinforcement program in a public school: A replication and systematic analysis. *Journal of Applied Behavior Analysis, 2,* 3–13.

Phillips, E. L. (1968). Achievement place: Token reinforcement procedures in a home-style rehabilitation setting for "pre-delinquent" boys. *Journal of Applied Behavior Analysis, 1,* 213–223.

Powell, J., Martindale, A., & Kulp, S. (1975). An evaluation of time-sampling measures of behavior. *Journal of Applied Behavior Analysis, 8,* 443–469.

Powell, J., Martindale, A., Kulp, S., Martindale, A., & Bowman, R. (1977). Taking a closer look: Time-sampling and measurement error. *Journal of Applied Behavior Analysis, 10,* 325–332.

Robinson, P. W., Newby, T. J., & Ganzell, S. J. (1981). A token system for a class of under-achieving, hyperactive children. *Journal of Applied Behavior Analysis, 14,* 307–316.

Schmidt, G. W., & Ulrich, R. E. (1969). Effects of group contingent events on classroom noise. *Journal of Applied Behavior Analysis, 2,* 171–179.

Schutte, R. C., & Hopkins, B. L. (1970). The effects of teacher attention on following instructions in a kindergarten class. *Journal of Applied Behavior Analysis, 3,* 117–122.

Smith, J. B., Madsen, C. H., Jr., & Cipani, E. (1981). The effects of observational session length, method of recording and frequency of behavior on the reliability and accuracy of observational data. *Behavior Therapy, 12,* 565–569.

Thomas, D. R., Becker, W. C., & Armstrong, M. (1968). Production and elimination of disruptive classroom behavior by systematically varying teacher's behavior. *Journal of Applied Behavior Analysis, 1,* 35–45.

Wahler, R. G. (1969). Setting generality: Some specific and general effects of child behavior therapy. *Journal of Applied Behavior Analysis, 2,* 239–246.

Walker, H. M., & Buckley, N. K. (1968). The use of positive reinforcement in conditioning attending behavior. *Journal of Applied Behavior Analysis, 1,* 245–250.

Ward, M. H., & Baker, B. L. (1968). Reinforcement therapy in the classroom. *Journal of Applied Behavior Analysis, 1,* 323–328.

Zeilberger, J., Sampen, S. E., & Sloane, H. N. (1968). Modification of a child's problem behavior in the home with the mother as therapist. *Journal of Applied Behavior Analysis, 1,* 47–53.

Zimmerman, E. H., Zimmerman, J., & Russell, C. D. (1969). Differential effects of token reinforcement on instruction—Following behavior in retarded students instructed as a group. *Journal of Applied Behavior Analysis, 2,* 101–112.

# 3    Basics of Single-Case Designs

Single-case designs constitute a prominent and practical methodology for educational personnel to demonstrate a functional relationship between student behavior (dependent variable) and changes in instructional and environmental strategies (independent variable). These designs, like group experimental designs, actively manipulate the treatment (or independent) variable to allow for cause and effect conclusions.

Often people have a misconception about single-case designs. The term *single-case* seems to suggest that such research is conducted with only one participant. Nothing could be further from the truth! Single-case designs usually utilize more than one participant in a research study. Some studies use as few as 2 or 3 participants, while others have whole classrooms of 20–30 students serving as participants. The term refers more to the way the data is collected than to the actual number of participants in the study.

Single-case designs have three distinctive characteristics: (1) repeated measurements of the same behavior within a single experimental condition; (2) implementation of each treatment or experimental condition across each participant; and (3) the fact that the individual participant serves as the basis for a comparison of experimental effects (called a within-participant analysis). While these characteristics were briefly reviewed in chapter 1, the present discussion will provide greater detail.

## CHARACTERISTICS OF SINGLE-CASE RESEARCH DESIGNS

### Questions to Ponder

- Why would you want someone to judge some performance of yours in a repeated fashion? What advantages would accrue to you? What advantages with regard to an accurate assessment of your performance might such a judgment yield?
- Do you prefer single-case designs that test each experimental condition across each participant or group designs in which each participant receives a different experimental condition? Why?
- Can group designs detect whether a treatment works for some people and not for others? Why or why not? How does a single-case design detect individual differences with regard to a given treatment?

## Repeated Measurements of Behavior

The first characteristic involves collecting data repeatedly on the same behavior (dependent variable) over a period of time. For instance, if one were to target student out-of-seat behavior in the classroom as the dependent variable in a research study, the measurement of this behavior would occur repeatedly across time. The students involved in the research study would be observed during a number of different sessions or days, in contrast to being observed just once. The collection of repeated measurements within a given experimental condition can be done through multiple sessions, days, weeks, or even blocks of trials. However, each new session, day, week, or block of trials (whatever is being used) should represent another data point on a graph.

Why is it necessary to collect repeated measures of student or class behavior when engaging in single-case research? Suppose I am interested in determining how friendly you are toward your fellow classmates. I define friendliness for the purposes of this experiment to be the number of times you smile, nod, or say something pleasant to people as you walk from one class to another. I decide to collect observational data. If I am using a group research design, one score for each participant is often sufficient. I will watch you once to determine the number of times you smile at people while you are walking the hallway to the next class you have. I note that you only smile once at someone. In relation to a classification system I have devised, based on this one observation, I conclude that you are not very friendly. Upon being told of the results, you indicate that normally you are very friendly. However, on that day you had some cough or tickle in your throat, which discouraged you from engaging in your usual friendly interactions with people. You assert that the one observation I made of you did not capture your usual pattern of behavior. You argue that I have gathered an inaccurate estimate of your behavior, leading to conclusions that are not warranted.

Upon reflection, I view your logic as having substance. You convince me that I should observe you more often in this venue and that the resulting data will be different. I do so unobtrusively (without your being aware of the times when I observe), and the following data result (see Table 3.1).

As it turns out, you were right! Measuring this behavior over a period of time has yielded a more accurate picture of your level of friendliness. You really are a friendly and popular individual! Using one day of data resulted in a gross underestimate of your level of friendliness.

This hypothetical example is a good illustration of the need to collect repeated measures of the target behavior in a given condition. Research that collects one score for each participant runs a greater risk of producing an inaccurate picture of each student's typical behavior. Repeated measurements of behavior within an experimental condition allow for a more accurate estimate and analysis of the level of behavior. Determining the level of behavior across time provides a more accurate picture of each individual participant.

How long is long enough? In the above example, making six observations over 6 separate days made the obtained data more representative. If I watched you three or four times each day for just 2 days, the resulting data might be less than representative of your usual level of behavior. You might be particularly withdrawn on these 2 days (or, at the other extreme, particularly happy about something). Hence the data resulting from a short time frame may be less accurate than the data resulting from a longer time frame. Therefore, measuring behavior over a period of time usually yields the best results, in terms of being representative of your behavior.

## Table 3.1

### FREQUENCY OF SMILING ACROSS FIVE ADDITIONAL OBSERVATION SESSIONS

| Day | 1 | 2 | 3 | 4 | 5 | 6 |
|---|---|---|---|---|---|---|
| Frequency | 1 | 6 | 5 | 8 | 4 | 6 |

Here is another example illustrating the need for continued repeated measurement in an elementary school setting. A hypothetical third-grade teacher, Mrs. Taggert, has a classroom management problem she wants to address. Several students (R.T., S.V., and D.L.) in her class have difficulty staying on task during silent reading time. They get distracted easily and sometimes begin conversing with each other while other students are trying to read. Mrs. Taggert wants a plan to address their on-task behavior during silent reading time. A successful plan could help these three students and make the classroom more conducive to silent reading time for other students. Mrs. Taggert observes the three students, using a time sampling interval recording system, for 3 days during the 20-minute silent reading period. The resulting levels of on-task behavior for each student are given in Table 3.2.

Mrs. Taggert reviews the data. She feels that something is not quite right. While she knows that R.T. has a problem staying on task, his percentage of on-task behavior is lower than she expected. Mrs. Taggert feels that R.T.'s level of on-task behavior is not that low on a consistent basis. To ensure a more accurate measurement of his level, she decides to collect another 4 days of data on on-task behavior (see Table 3.3).

**Table 3.2**

**PERCENTAGES OF ON-TASK BEHAVIOR FOR THREE STUDENTS**

| STUDENT | DAY 1 | DAY 2 | DAY 3 |
|---------|-------|-------|-------|
| R.T. | 25 | 17 | 19 |
| S.V. | 55 | 60 | 45 |
| D.L. | 27 | 30 | 44 |

**Table 3.3**

**ADDITIONAL DATA COLLECTION FOR THREE STUDENTS (PERCENTAGES)**

| STUDENT | DAY 1 | DAY 2 | DAY 3 | DAY 4 | DAY 5 | DAY 6 | DAY 7 |
|---------|-------|-------|-------|-------|-------|-------|-------|
| R.T. | 25 | 17 | 19 | 45 | 54 | 35 | 32 |
| S.V. | 55 | 60 | 45 | 48 | 68 | 44 | 50 |
| D.L. | 27 | 30 | 44 | 29 | 62 | 48 | 52 |

As Mrs. Taggert suspected, R.T.'s on-task rate during the next 4 days is elevated above the rates obtained on the first 3 days. R.T. is still in need of improvement, but the latter 4 days provide a more accurate picture of the extent of his deficit. On some days his rate is very low, for example, 17%, but on many days he is in the 32%–54% range.

In summary, collecting repeated measures of the dependent variable across a period of time allows the researcher to study and capture each participant's variability in exhibiting the behavior being measured as the dependent variable. This is essential in the methodology of single-case designs.

## Multiple Experimental Conditions Across Each Participant

The second characteristic of single-case designs is that multiple experimental conditions (all having repeated measurements) are implemented across each participant (Bailey & Bostow, 1981; Hersen & Barlow, 1976). Single-case designs can compare several different experimental conditions, as can group designs. However, in a single-case design, each participant is exposed to each experimental condition. This allows for a comparison of any two experimental conditions with regard to behavior to be made for each individual participant. The determination of effectiveness is made for each individual participant (thus, within-participant effects can be studied).

The control condition in many single-case designs is called the baseline condition. It is a measure of the target behavior or skill before any formal treatment or instructional condition is imposed. Most single-case designs utilize this condition to allow for a comparison of the rates of behavior before and after the designated treatment strategy is deployed. Data are collected repeatedly within the baseline condition, as is the case with other experimental conditions.

Figure 3.1 illustrates a single-case design with hypothetical data on the number of cooperative responses of a withdrawn fourth-grade student during cooperative learning sessions. While this example illustrates a comparison between just two conditions, other single-case designs are capable of comparing more than two experimental conditions.

As you can see, the teacher in this example measured the number of cooperative behaviors displayed by the student across 30 sessions (raw frequency data are provided in appendix B). The data collection of the same dependent variable occurs across each experimental condition. The

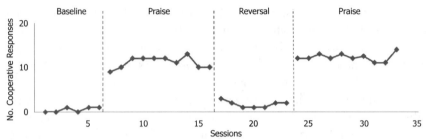

**Figure 3.1** Number of cooperative responses.

teacher compared the effectiveness of two conditions in this research study: (1) the baseline condition; and (2) teacher praise. The baseline condition involved the measurement of the number of cooperative behaviors exhibited under the existent conditions. When there is no formal intervention, the baseline condition is often a hodgepodge of strategies. In this case, the baseline condition might represent an ever-changing attempt to try to get more cooperative responses from the participant. Measurement of the baseline condition continued for six sessions, with a rate of cooperative behavior between zero and one being displayed during the observation period. The teacher then changed the experiment to involve teacher praise for cooperative behavior (labeled "praise" in Figure 3.1). This switch in conditions was initiated in Session 7 and lasted until Session 16.

In the teacher praise condition, the student was praised by the teacher whenever he engaged in cooperative behavior with another student. Instances of showing work to peers, sharing work with peers, or making positive comments to a peer were praised by the teacher. The teacher implemented this intervention for 10 days. The result was an increase in the student's level of cooperative behavior, with a range between 9 and 13 instances during the observation period. When the teacher saw that a stable level of cooperative behavior had been established in this condition, she then returned to the baseline condition (this return is marked "reversal" in Figure 3.1) for a 7-day period. In this reversal condition (from Session 17 through Session 23), she stopped providing praise when the withdrawn student engaged in cooperative behavior. This was done to determine what effect it would have on the high rate previously established in the praise condition. Figure 3.1 reveals a decrease in the level of cooperative behavior during the reversal condition, with no day seeing more than 3 incidences of cooperative behavior. She then reinstituted the intervention plan, beginning with Session 24, that is, praising cooperative behavior, and continued this treatment until the end of the data collection in Session 33. With the return of this intervention, the rate of the cooperative behavior went back to high levels.

It is important to note in this example that the student was exposed to each experimental condition, that is, baseline and teacher praise. As Figure 3.1 makes evident, the effects of teacher praise on cooperative behavior were significant. This study demonstrates a functional relationship between the independent variable (treatment vs. baseline) and the dependent variable (cooperative behavior).

## Each Individual Participant Is the Basis for Analysis

This characteristic is probably most reflective of single-case designs. In the hypothetical study discussed above, the comparison of experimental conditions (e.g., baseline vs. praise) is made within the same individual student. In examining the graphed data, the level of cooperative behavior for the two experimental conditions is compared for that student.

Single-case designs measure within-participant experimental effects (Bailey & Bostow, 1981), in contrast to the measurement of between-participant effects in the case of group designs. Why is this important? Some treatments may be effective for some students but not for others. If you average the results across an entire group, individual differences in treatment effectiveness are lost. In contrast, if each individual participant serves as the basis for comparison at each level of the independent variable, individual variation with respect to each condition will become apparent. In this manner, you can determine whether a given intervention is effective for some students but maybe not for others.

While many single-case studies produce individual participant data, one need not restrict data collection to individual participants. Single-case designs can also be used for entire groups or classes (Cooper et al., 2007). You simply treat the group as an individual unit. For example, Figure 3.1 could show an entire class's rate of cooperative behavior. During each session, the researcher would collect the rate of cooperative behavior exhibited by anyone in the class and plot that cumulative sum on the graph. The changes in experimental condition would be in effect for all members of the class. The teacher praise condition would involve the teacher praising anyone in the class who exhibited a cooperative response to another student. The essential requirement in a single-case design is to present the data across all experimental conditions for the group being studied.

## REQUISITES FOR COLLECTING SINGLE-CASE RESEARCH DATA

### Questions to Ponder

- How do you determine whether you have a sufficient number of data points in a given experimental condition?
- Using the graphing conventions and rules listed in appendix C, please graph the hypothetical data of a student with two conditions, baseline and treatment. The dependent variable is the percentage of correct steps for an algebra problem that has six steps involved in the calculation.

In the previous section, it was stressed that repeated measurements increase the accuracy of the estimate of the level of behavior within an experimental condition. How do you know when you have collected enough data on a condition? Figures 3.2 and 3.3 illustrate the utility of collecting a sufficient number of repeated measurements within an experimental condition. These graphs depict hypothetical data on the percentage of off-task behavior for a fourth-grade class during independent seat work in math.

Figure 3.2 presents the percentage of off-task behavior in this hypothetical class after two sessions of data collection. It shows that off-task behavior in the first session was 25%, while the second session resulted in an off-task percentage of 75%. Is this enough data to make one feel confident that one has a good idea of what the class's level of off-task

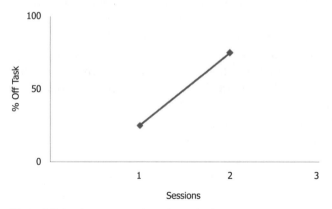

**Figure 3.2** Inadequate number of repeated measurements within an experimental condition.

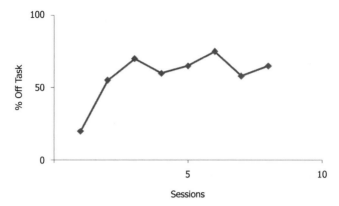

**Figure 3.3** Adequate number of measurements within a condition.

behavior is? Is this class really adequate at sustaining attention during independent seat work (e.g., Session 1)? Or is the class more like the data point depicted for Session 2 (e.g., 75%)? If the data collection is terminated at this point, the estimate of the level of behavior will probably be inaccurate. In Figure 3.3, a different researcher in another class collects data during six more sessions after the first two sessions. The resulting hypothetical data reveal a greater stability.

Figure 3.3 demonstrates the utility of collecting additional data during measurement of the baseline condition. The data from the first session (i.e., 20% off task) were highly atypical of the performance of this class (the raw data for Figure 3.3 are found in appendix D). With the addition of six more baseline sessions than those collected in Figure 3.2, it is apparent that the percentage of off-task behavior of this class is closer to between 55% and 75%. The mean for this group of sessions data is 58%, far above what the estimate would have been had this researcher stopped at two sessions of data collection. As Figures 3.2 and 3.3 illustrate, collecting too few data points within an experimental condition can produce an inaccurate estimate of the level of behavior.

## Stability of Data

How many data points are sufficient to obtain a stable pattern of data? The stability of the data is defined and demonstrated by a leveling off of the rate of response at a certain range (Bailey & Bostow, 1981; Cooper, Heron, & Heward, 2007). Stability allows for some type of prediction about what the data would have been if the experimental condition had been measured for a longer period of time. The number of data points necessary to obtain stability within a given experimental condition is a function of the displayed variability of the behavior. If the data displayed are highly variable, more data need to be collected so as to ensure that you have accurately captured the level of the behavior. However, if the data show little variability (a close range of scores), then there is no need to collect extended data within that condition to obtain a stable rate.

A hypothetical student in a special education class for adolescents with severe problem behaviors is reported by his teacher to engage in a high level of disruptive behavior. He will throw pencils at other students, make unauthorized comments during seat work, and get out of his seat and begin conversations with other students. His teacher, Mr. Peak, collects a baseline level of such disruptive behaviors. He wants to make sure that he captures the level of behavior so as to determine accurately the extent of the problem before imposing an intervention. Figure 3.4 hypothesizes a rate of response for this student's disruptive behavior across 10 days under the baseline condition.

The graph in Figure 3.4 depicts the range of this child's daily disruptive behaviors as being between 5 and 8 occurrences. Is it reasonable to assume that if data were collected for another 5 days, the rate of disruptive behaviors would be in this range of 5 to 8 occurrences or close to it? Given this stable set of data, it would seem highly improbable that the next five data points following day 10 would show a dramatic change in the range to 10–14 destructive acts. It also seems improbable that the range would decrease substantially (e.g., to 0 to 2), given that the same baseline condition was present. One would only consider

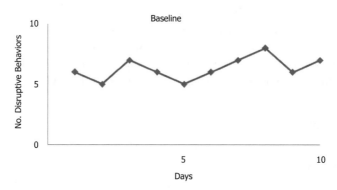

**Figure 3.4** Stable rate of data within a condition.
*Note.* The actual frequency per session is 6, 5, 7, 6, 5, 6, 7, 8, 6, and 7.

this possibility if, in one of the first 10 days, the rate had dropped to such a low level. Given the data collected over the 10-day period, we can be reasonably sure that future rates of disruptive behavior under the same baseline condition would be in or near the same range.

Unstable data within a condition do not allow the researcher or practitioner to be able to predict, with any assurance, a future rate of response under the same baseline or experimental conditions (Bailey & Bostow, 1981). Suppose the data collected for a class's disruptive behavior during a reading group's activity for the first 4 days had been as presented in Figure 3.5.

At the end of Day 4, the data obtained cannot allow anyone to predict with any degree of assurance the range of behavior in the baseline condition. It is quite possible that further data collection in the baseline condition would yield either a higher rate or a lower rate, in another seven sessions. If seven more baseline sessions had occurred, data illustrated by the closed triangles could result. Do you see the problem that occurs with a short baseline condition (i.e., just four days)? The teacher would have overestimated this child's real level of disruptive behavior. Of course, data at the other extreme could also have resulted, as illustrated by the closed boxes. As the boxes show, the first 4 days could also have underestimated the rate of disruptive behaviors. Both possibilities show that 4 days of baseline data are inadequate. With such a small data set, the potential for inaccurately determining the true level of disruptive behavior exists.

Examine the following three graphs (Figures 3.6, 3.7, and 3.8) involving hypothesized data sets. The hypothetical data in Figure 3.6 provides

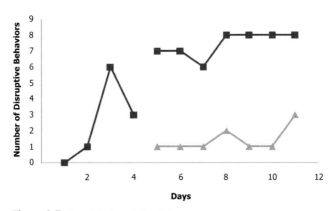

**Figure 3.5** Possible trends in data.

the rate of inappropriate social interactions for 12 sessions. While the first 4 days showed great variability in the frequency of this behavior, the last 8 days provided a stable level of this behavior. But reaching a level of stability required data collection to be extended to 12 sessions. Figures 3.7 and 3.8 show that smaller amounts of data need to be collected (seven and six sessions respectively) as a result of the fact that the levels of this behavior were closer together across all the sessions.

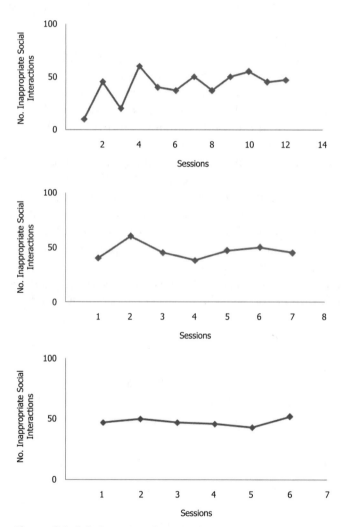

**Figures 3.6–3.8** Examples of repeated measurements within a condition.

In summary, the number of data points needed under a given experimental condition is a function of the variability of the behavior. If the behavior is highly variable, with high rates of responding in some sessions and low rates of responding in other sessions, more data need to be collected before the particular experimental condition is terminated and a new condition is initiated.

## Trending in the Data

Trending and stability are related, in that one cannot usually have stable data and also have data that trend. Trending can occur at the end of the experimental condition. Figure 3.9 shows a downward trend in the rate of student outbursts during teacher lectures in a hypothetical 10th-grade classroom. The data are plotted across each week, as a cumulative measure. During Week 1, 24 total outbursts occurred. In Week 2, a total of 35 outbursts was recorded by the teacher. Later the trend became a downward one.

Note that the data are showing a decreasing trend in the number of outbursts from the student, starting with Week 5. If a treatment condition is implemented in Week 9, and a lower rate is obtained for the next five weeks, can one conclude that the treatment has produced the change in rate? Unfortunately, due to the existing downward trend, one cannot. The teacher should continue to collect data until this trend levels off or begins to ascend.

Not all trending data prohibit changing experimental conditions (Bailey & Bostow, 1981). If the data in Figure 3.9 depicted a base level consisting of the number of pages read in the class each week,

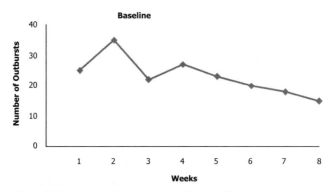

**Figure 3.9** Downward trend in baseline condition.

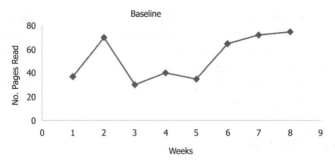

**Figure 3.10** Upward trend in baseline condition.

then the downward trend displayed would not be problematic, since the trend with an effective intervention program would be in the opposite direction. In other words, if the trend in a given condition is in the direction opposite to that of the intended effect of an intervention, one can terminate data collection without jeopardizing the clarity of the data set.

The opposite of a downward trend is an upward trend. Figure 3.10 presents data on the number of pages read per week in a fourth-grade class participating in a literacy program. The trend depicted is upward at Week 6 and beyond (the cautions delineated earlier are also applicable here). If the intervention is expected to increase the number of pages read, the researcher will have to continue collecting data until the data in Figure 3.10 trend downward.

## DETERMINING AN EXPERIMENTAL EFFECT

### Questions to Ponder
- What advantages does the collection of baseline data afford the applied researcher?
- Why is trending in the baseline a problem for the interpretation of results?
- Why does significant overlap make an interpretation of the treatment effect ambiguous?

Comparison of data obtained under different experimental conditions is done through a visual analysis of the data presented in chart or graph form. Unlike group designs, where the data are subjected to a statistical test to determine whether there is a difference between conditions, single-case studies rely on substantial visually apparent differences. In single-case designs, the magnitude of the difference must be visually apparent and noticeable.

The determination of a substantial difference between the baseline and experimental conditions is made when the graphed data meet the following criteria (Bailey & Bostow, 1981; Cooper et al., 2007): (1) change in the mean score (in the desired direction) between the conditions being compared; (2) little or no overlap between conditions; and (3) less variability in treatment conditions than in less effective control or other conditions.

A change in the mean score for each condition must be visually apparent. Table 3.4 shows two charts presenting 10 days' worth of data in Condition A and the same in Condition B. The difference in the means is apparent upon a simple visual examination of the data under each condition. The means are given in the right-hand columns for both conditions (47% and 19% respectively).

While the difference in the mean can be examined using tabled data, determining whether the difference in the two conditions meets the other two criteria is best done with a graph. An illustration of a significant difference between two conditions (baseline and treatment) is provided in a hypothetical example with on-task behavior as the dependent variable. The tabled data is provided in Table 3.5. In the upper panel of the table, the percentage of on-task behavior during the 10 days of the

## Table 3.4

**EXAMPLE OF SIGNIFICANT DIFFERENCE BETWEEN TWO CONDITIONS IN TERMS OF THE MEAN SCORE**

| | | | | | DAYS | | | | | | |
|---|---|---|---|---|---|---|---|---|---|---|---|
| **CONDITION A** | 1 | 2 | 3 | 4 | 5 | 6 | 7 | 8 | 9 | 10 | |
| | 35 | 45 | 60 | 50 | 50 | 42 | 44 | 50 | 50 | 35 | Mean about 47% |

| | | | | | DAYS | | | | | | |
|---|---|---|---|---|---|---|---|---|---|---|---|
| **CONDITION B** | 1 | 2 | 3 | 4 | 5 | 6 | 7 | 8 | 9 | 10 | |
| | 25 | 15 | 30 | 10 | 27 | 22 | 14 | 0 | 30 | 15 | Mean about 19% |

baseline condition is given. In the lower panel, the percentage of on-task behavior during the 8 days of the treatment condition is found.

When these data points are graphed on an *x*, *y* coordinate plane, Figure 3.11 results.

The baseline condition depicts the 10 days of data collection, with a range between 25% and 60% on task. The mean (arithmetical average) for this condition is about 44%. The treatment condition depicts the 8 days of data collection, with a range between 60% and 90% on task. The mean for this condition is about 79%. But what about the other two criteria? There is little overlap between conditions. Only one data point in each condition overlaps, and that is 60% for on-task behavior for the baseline condition on the third day and the same rate for the treatment condition on Day 11.

Substantial overlap does not allow one to judge that one condition is significantly different from the other. The graph in Figure 3.12 depicts

Table 3.5

**RAW DATA ON OFF-TASK BEHAVIOR (PERCENTAGES)**

| | DAYS | | | | | | | | | |
|---|---|---|---|---|---|---|---|---|---|---|
| **BASELINE** | 1 | 2 | 3 | 4 | 5 | 6 | 7 | 8 | 9 | 10 |
| | 25 | 45 | 60 | 50 | 37 | 42 | 44 | 50 | 50 | 35 |

| | DAYS | | | | | | | |
|---|---|---|---|---|---|---|---|---|
| **TREATMENT** | 11 | 12 | 13 | 14 | 15 | 16 | 17 | 18 |
| | 60 | 80 | 80 | 85 | 80 | 90 | 75 | 80 |

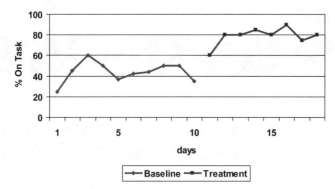

**Figure 3.11** Data display for two conditions, baseline and treatment.

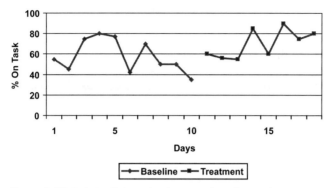

**Figure 3.12** Substantial overlap between baseline and treatment conditions.

substantial overlap. While there does appear to be a difference in the means for the two conditions, there is too much of an overlap between the data points in the baseline condition and those in the treatment condition. A visual inspection would not conclude that the treatment program produced higher rates of on-task behavior than the baseline condition.

It is one thing to obtain a difference between two experimental conditions, as the graph in Figure 3.12 shows with respect to on-task behavior. But is the difference sizable enough to be noticeable? In the graph, we see that the intervention condition produced sizable gains in on-task behavior. Focusing on interventions and treatments that produce a sizable noticeable change in student behavior will lead to more powerful technologies, both behavioral and instructional. Concurrently, treatments that produce weak effects will be removed from the evidence base.

## GROUP VERSUS SINGLE-CASE EXPERIMENTAL DESIGNS

### Question to Ponder

- Discuss the differences between group designs and single-case designs.

There are many compelling reasons why educational researchers should use single-case designs and not group designs in validating treatment efficacy. The major differences between group and single-case designs are depicted in Table 3.6.

Table 3.6

### DIFFERENCES BETWEEN GROUP AND SINGLE-CASE DESIGNS

| METHODOLOGICAL ISSUE | GROUP DESIGNS | SINGLE-CASE DESIGNS |
|---|---|---|
| Treatment provided for all participants in study? | No | Yes; participants serve as their own control |
| Treatment compared with nontreatment for each participant? | No | Yes |
| Data on magnitude of change for each participant? | No | Yes |
| Concern with reliability of one score to represent effect of experimental condition? | Yes | No |
| Large number of participants needed? | Yes | No; possible study variable of interest (student behavior) in your class |
| Random samples from target population needed? | Yes | No; can possibly use students in your own classroom (or from one class) |
| Strength of generalizability of study results to others in population? | Moderate | Weak (with just one study, direct and systematic replication needed) |

The withholding of treatment from a number of participants in the control condition is problematic in group designs. This does not apply to single-case designs. If the participant is in the baseline or control condition for some period of time, treatment will be implemented subsequent to the baseline data reaching stability.

A related issue is the comparison of treatment effects within each participant. In a single-case design, no comparison is made between one student's baseline and another student's treatment condition(s). Rather, each participant will be subjected to both the control and experimental conditions. This will yield an analysis of relative effects for each participant. The protocol used in between-participant group designs is the opposite, since one participant in Group A receives Treatment A while another participant in Group B receives Treatment B. Using such a methodology, it is not known how the respective participant would have performed in the other experimental condition. It is therefore impossible to determine the effects of each experimental condition on each individual participant. A hypothetical example can illustrate this problem.

A hypothetical researcher uses a group design to determine whether self-monitoring of outbursts is more effective than teacher monitoring of student outbursts. Ten students were randomly assigned to the self-monitoring group and another 10 were randomly assigned to the teacher-monitoring group (see Table 3.7).

Table 3.8 depicts each student in the two groups and the number of outbursts that occurred on the day data were scheduled to be collected on the rate of outbursts.

The data are analyzed by comparing the means of the two groups through various statistical procedures. The mean for the self-monitoring group is 5.22, and for the other group it is 2.33. If such a difference is statistically significant (i.e., not due to chance), then one would conclude that teacher monitoring is better than self-monitoring in reducing outbursts. But can this be done for each individual student?

In examining the data above, can we know how student B.P. would have done under the teacher-monitoring condition? Similarly, what score would student A.B. have achieved under self-monitoring? Can we be reasonably confident that random assignment of participants to one of two groups equated the groups on relevant variables? Maybe in

## Table 3.7

**PARTICIPANT ASSIGNMENT TO GROUPS: SELF-MONITORING VERSUS TEACHER MONITORING**

| SELF-MONITORING GROUP | TEACHER-MONITORING GROUP |
|---|---|
| R.T. | B.F. |
| B.B. | G.M. |
| V.H. | T.T. |
| F.E. | A.B. |
| B.A. | L.D. |
| Y.F. | L.C. |
| V.C. | C.S. |
| G.G. | K.B. |
| B.P. | O.G. |

Table 3.8

**SELF-MONITORED AND TEACHER-MONITORED GROUPS: NUMBERS OF OUTBURSTS (IN PARENTHESES)**

| SELF-MONITORING GROUP | TEACHER-MONITORING GROUP |
| --- | --- |
| R.T. (2) | B.F. (0) |
| B.B. (8) | G.M. (2) |
| V.H. (4) | T.T. (1) |
| F.E. (4) | A.B. (4) |
| B.A. (2) | L.D. (0) |
| Y.F. (8) | L.C. (0) |
| V.C. (6) | C.S. (7) |
| G.G. (6) | K.B. (3) |
| B.P. (7) | O.G. (4) |

the study of peas, random assignment might work with low numbers of participants per group, but not with people! Single-case designs control for this problem by subjecting each student to each experimental condition. In a single-case research design, each participant experiences each experimental condition. The method by which this occurs depends on the exact design that is selected (see chapter 4).

Group designs collect one score for each participant in the experimental condition(s) and the control condition. As a result, the reliability of that score as being representative of the individual's behavior under that condition is of concern. Single-case designs involve repeated measurements of behavior within a given experimental condition for each student. Thus, the reliability or consistency of a single score is a nonissue.

The generalizability of the results depicted in Table 3.6 is often cited as an advantage of group designs over single-case designs. Given that group designs usually involve more students, the external validity of their results would seem to be better. However, both methodologies really require direct and systematic replication of results for external validity to be established. Even in group designs with 10 participants in each treatment condition, it is necessary to establish that such results would occur in other university research laboratories, with other experimenters, and with other students throughout the country.

## SUMMARY

Single-case research designs provide a very practical methodology for educational settings. The features of such designs make them more appropriate than group designs for many educational research projects in classrooms. Single-case designs have three distinctive characteristics: (1) repeated measurements of the same behavior within a single experimental condition; (2) implementation of each treatment or experimental condition across each participant; and (3) analysis of within-participant effects. Treatment effects are determined by identifying visually apparent differences in the dependent variable between experimental conditions, provided that each condition meets the requirement for stability and lack of trending.

## REFERENCES

Bailey, J. S., & Bostow, D. E. (1981). *Research methods in applied behavior analysis.* Tallahassee, FL: Copy Grafix.

Cooper, J. O., Heron, T. F., & Heward, W. L. (2007). *Applied behavior analysis* (2nd ed.). Columbus, OH: Merrill/Prentice Hall.

Hersen, M., & Barlow, D. H. (1976). *Single-case experimental designs: Strategies in studying behavior change.* New York: Pergamon Press.

# Single-Case Designs

There are various single-case designs. Two factors that can differ within each type of single-case design are the following: (1) the number of experimental conditions tested; and (2) the ability of the design to validate the change in the independent variable as the causal agent in the change in the dependent variable (a demonstration of a functional relationship). Some single-case designs compare only two different experimental conditions; others may compare multiple conditions. Single-case designs also vary with respect to their ability to validate the cause of the change in behavior as the manipulation of the independent variable. Some single-case designs do not allow for a causal interpretation, whereas other types of designs allow for a causal interpretation. The latter achieve this by replicating experimental conditions to determine whether effects are replicable and thereby to isolate the independent variable as the causal variable.

## AB AND ADDITIVE DESIGNS

### Questions to Ponder
- Do these designs (AB or additive) allow for a cause-and-effect analysis of the experimental effects? Why or why not?
- What is a baseline condition?

- What are the two functions of collecting baseline data?
- What are the two limiting conditions of an additive design?
- Why is experimental control not demonstrated in an AB design?
- Do AB designs involve the testing of two or more experimental conditions?
- What constitutes an additive design?
- What are sequence effects in an additive design?
- Why does the use of an ABC design not allow for a cause-and-effect analysis of the experimental effects?
- One of the functions of baseline data is to determine the extent of the target behavior. Why is this essential?
- Why do sequence effects make interpretation of the data difficult when a treatment effect is rendered in the C (or D) condition?
- Describe a hypothetical study that uses an additive design labeled ABCD. What experimental conditions would be implemented, in sequential order, and what would be the dependent variable?
- If the data within each condition do not overlap, more credibility might be given to the behavior change as an experimental effect in an ABC design. Can you think of a possible example of such a circumstance?

## Brief Description of AB Designs

The AB design involves two experimental conditions, the first condition designated as A, and the second condition designated as B. Generally, the first condition is the baseline condition, and then, after a sufficient number of data points are collected, a treatment procedure is implemented as a second condition. The baseline condition (or control condition) is generally the measurement of the target behavior before any treatment procedure (another experimental condition) is implemented. Most research and evaluation projects begin by collecting baseline data on the target behavior. The baseline condition serves two functions: It determines the extent of the problem (by measuring the behavior before any treatment is initiated), and it allows for a comparison of treatment results obtained in the second condition with data obtained in Condition A. The teacher or researcher implements a baseline condition until stability is reached and there is no trending in the data. Therefore, the AB design is the analysis of two experimental conditions (baseline and treatment) in sequential fashion. A comparison between the rates of the target behavior under baseline and treatment conditions can be made. The experimental or treatment effect is determined by this comparison. An effect is inferred if there is a sizable decrease in the level of the target behavior from the baseline to the treatment condition.

## Examples of AB Designs

### It's Story Time!

How would an AB design be used in a classroom research project? A hypothetical first-grade teacher has a class that frequently exhibits inappropriate requests and remarks at story time. She classifies these behaviors as inappropriate outbursts. The teacher records the frequency of inappropriate outbursts over an 8-day period (see the baseline condition in Figure 4.1).

The baseline data (Phase A) in Figure 4.1 reveal that the rate of this behavior is at problematic levels. It ranges between 6 occurrences (in the best story time session) and a high of 14 outbursts in Session 3. Once the baseline data have stabilized, the teacher implements a different condition. In Session 9, she implements a treatment strategy that involves two components: (1) a review of the behavior rules for story time; and (2) the use of 1 minute of earned preferred activity time in return for each 5-minute block in which no outbursts occur during story time. This treatment strategy constitutes the second experimental condition (Phase B). It is visually apparent that the number of outbursts has dropped considerably following the implementation of the treatment condition. The first session of treatment resulted in only 5 outbursts in story time. Subsequently, the rate of outbursts was either

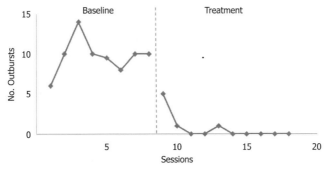

**Figure 4.1** AB design.

at 1 occurrence per session (Sessions 10 and 13) or at 0. Note that there is no overlap of data points between the two conditions. What a difference this treatment has made to the rate of this problem behavior! Using the AB design, the teacher has evaluated the effects of this two-component treatment package on outbursts during story time in her first-grade class.

## Can We Be Quiet!

A hypothetical fourth-grade class has difficulty becoming quiet and getting ready to listen when the teacher, Mrs. Parker, wants to switch instructional activities. Mrs. Parker wants the students in her class to demonstrate more appropriate transition behavior. This target problem behavior constitutes the dependent variable. Appropriate transition behavior is defined as the student being quiet and facing the teacher within 10 seconds after a transition to another activity is announced (e.g., "Class, look at me. We are going to switch activities"). Mrs. Parker collects the data by counting the number of students who demonstrate this target behavior within 10 seconds of each transition announcement. The total number of students displaying appropriate transition behavior within the 10-second limit is obtained, as is the total number of students. Therefore, for each transition activity, Mrs. Parker obtains a percentage of appropriate transition behavior for the class. She then computes a daily average percentage of appropriate transition behavior. Her baseline involves the current strategy she deploys: constant reminders to "Show me you are ready to learn." The resulting data, presented in Figure 4.2, show a low rate of appropriate transition behavior each day.

Following the 10 days of baseline data collection, Mrs. Parker deploys a treatment strategy to address the problem. She decides to put the percentage of appropriate transition behavior for each transition activity on the board, thus incorporating a component of public feedback to the class. Additionally, for each transition in which the class achieves a 60% or higher level of appropriate transition behavior, everyone in the class earns two points. The teacher continues to collect data on the target behavior during this second condition. The data presented in Figure 4.2 illustrate the mean percentage of students exhibiting the target behavior across all transitions for each day. These data show that the treatment strategy produced a change in the mean and level of behavior (no data overlap).

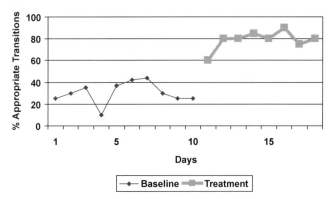

**Figure 4.2** AB design depicting significant difference between baseline and treatment conditions.

## Research Example

An AB design with follow-up assessments was used to monitor the school refusal behavior of a female preschool child in Queensland, Australia (Gosschalk, 2004). A functional behavioral assessment identified the crying and complaining behavior exhibited by the child as functional in getting her mother's attention. When she engaged in such behavior, the mother would not send her to school that day. The dependent variable was attending and remaining at school for the entire day. Baseline (Condition A) data for three weeks revealed that the girl did not attend school at all during that period.

Treatment (Condition B) was provided in the home setting and focused on increasing the length of time the girl would be separated from her mother. This involved her mother being out of sight of the girl while at home for increasing time periods, with reinforcement. The treatment condition was continued for 30 weeks. A significant change accrued. The last 3 weeks resulted in 100% attendance at school (and remaining there). Two follow-up periods of 3 weeks, conducted at 4 and 12 months after the treatment program was discontinued, revealed continued success. For all 6 weeks, 100% attendance was recorded.

## Steps to Conducting Research Using AB Designs

The steps to conducting single-case research using an AB design are given in Table 4.1.

Table 4.1

### STEPS TO CONDUCTING RESEARCH USING AN AB DESIGN

1. Identify the dependent variable.
2. Define the dependent variable.
3. Design the observation system, including length of sessions and data collectors.
4. Graph data frequently (daily or at every session).
5. Implement the baseline condition until stability is achieved.
6. Implement the treatment condition until stability is achieved.
7. Compare data across A and B conditions.

## Advantages of AB Designs

Too often in educational practice, methods or treatments are altered on the spur of the moment, without an analysis of what rate of behavior or effect is currently existent. The AB design uses the obtained baseline data to determine whether an implemented treatment (Condition B) was effective. By collecting baseline data prior to implementing an alternative treatment strategy, one can determine whether the designed treatment strategy worked better than the approaches that were being used in the baseline condition.

A major advantage of an AB design is its feasibility of use in everyday classrooms. Following the collection of baseline data, a treatment (believed to be effective) is implemented. With a change in the behavior (dependent variable), the teacher has solved the problem behavior or changed the skill level of the student. Such a procedure can certainly be used in situations where it may be necessary to prove that some treatment is producing progress in reducing an undesirable behavior or increasing an appropriate behavior or academic skill. It is well suited as a practical evaluation tool for the classroom teacher. It also serves well as a pilot project for a thesis or dissertation study.

## Limitation of AB Designs

Because the AB design does not replicate either of the experimental conditions, it fails to demonstrate experimental control of the independent variable. When the data from Figure 4.1 is examined, the significant change in behavior may be attributed to the change in experimental conditions (baseline to treatment), but unfortunately other changes cannot be ruled out (e.g., maturation, change in behavior due to the passage of time, participant expectation, sensitization to any treatment, etc.). The AB design generally does not support inferences regarding the change in behavior as a result of the change in the independent variable. For example, in the study on outbursts discussed above, one cannot conclude unambiguously that the treatment strategy resulted in the decrease in outbursts. A number of other factors might have changed concurrently with the change from the baseline condition to the treatment condition. As will be shown later, a replication of effects following a replication of conditions can rule out alternative explanations of the behavior change.

However, producing a very rapid change in behavior with the implementation of the second experimental condition (immediate onset of experimental effect) may add some credibility to a cause-and-effect conclusion. The best way, however, to obtain an unambiguous interpretation regarding independent variable effects is still to utilize another design that will allow valid cause-and-effect statements. Certainly, for teachers wishing to find out if some procedure is working, an AB design is a good start point. For a researcher, utilizing AB designs as good pilot work (whether one is engaged in research or evaluation studies) may possibly be a laudable use of these designs.

## Brief Description of Additive Designs

The additive design is an extension of the AB design. It involves adding a number of different experimental conditions (without replicating any of the previous experimental conditions). For example, if two additional conditions are implemented after the baseline condition, the design is called an ABC design. If four treatment conditions are implemented after the baseline condition (making a total of five conditions), then the additive design is ABCDE. In other words, each subsequent treatment condition is given the next letter in the alphabet; so, for example, five different conditions implemented in succession make up an ABCDE additive design.

The additive design allows for the implementation of a number of different conditions. The additive design is commonly employed when the experimental condition in an AB design does not obtain a desired effect and thus creates a need for another approach to be tried. For example, a researcher decides to examine the effectiveness of self-monitoring on three students' adherence to library study rules when using individual study carrels. The rules are as follows: (1) no talking while in a study carrel; (2) no more than five books from the library shelves to be used in the study carrel; and (3) all books to be put back in the shelving area before leaving the study carrel. The researcher implements a self-monitoring treatment following a baseline. The treatment does not result in a significant change in adherence to the three rules. This researcher adds an additional component to the self-monitoring, one of contingent access to the library carrel. The students must adhere to the rules in order to be able to use the study carrel the next library day. If they break a rule, they lose the carrel privilege the next library day and must use the regular tables for their study.

The design used in this study then becomes ABC (see Table 4.2).

## Examples of ABC Designs

### Reading Performance

The teacher of a hypothetical fourth-grade class is concerned about the low rate of words read correctly during oral reading sessions with students in one group in the class (the dolphin group). She collects baseline data on their reading performance. The baseline data measure the rate of words read correctly by each student in this group during the first 5 minutes of the session.

Figure 4.3 illustrates the sequential implementation of the baseline and the two succeeding conditions, in an ABC design. The number of words read correctly per minute in the baseline condition is low, between 5 and 10. Following the baseline condition, the treatment condition, which involves a simple correction strategy, produces an increase in the rate of words read correctly per minute, with 8 of the 10 sessions resulting in a higher rate than any session in the baseline condition. There is some overlap, but one can still conclude that Condition B has increased the rate of words per minute in comparison to Condition A. When the

Table 4.2

| SEQUENCE OF EXPERIMENTAL CONDITIONS IN AN ABC DESIGN | | |
|---|---|---|
| **CONDITION A** | **CONDITION B** | **CONDITION C** |
| Baseline | Self-monitoring | Earned study carrel privilege |

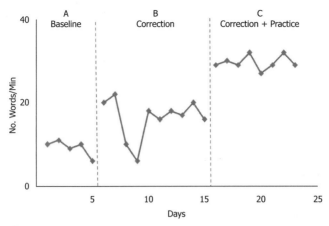

**Figure 4.3** Additive design.

teacher implements the next treatment condition, Condition C, that is, the correction strategy and additional practice, a higher level of words read per minute is achieved. The mean rate of words read correctly increases substantially over the previous condition (with no overlap).

## Can We Be Quiet!

Suppose Mrs. Parker, the hypothetical teacher depicted previously, used a strategy that did not work in the first treatment condition. After a baseline condition, she implements a "wrong" strategy and collects data on this strategy for 5 days. Her dependent variable is the number of students who are quiet and facing her after a transition is announced. This appropriate transition behavior has to occur within 10 seconds of the announcement. During this condition (B), Mrs. Parker provides warnings to the students who are not engaged in appropriate behavior 5 seconds after her initial request, "Show me you are ready." This strategy unfortunately does not generate any significant increase in the level of the class target behavior (see Figure 4.4).

In Condition C, Mrs. Parker deploys the Good Behavior Board Game (GBBG). She continues to collect data on the target behavior during this condition. The data in Figure 4.4 illustrate the mean percentage of students exhibiting the target behavior across all transitions for each day for all three conditions. The GBBG treatment strategy results in a significant change in the percentage of students demonstrating appropriate transition behavior for each day (with no overlap to baseline or first treatment condition).

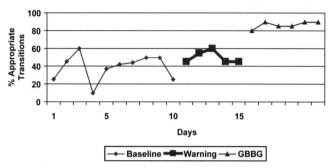

**Figure 4.4** ABC design.

## Research Example: Academic Responding

An ABC design with a follow-up period was used to determine whether a unique instructional management procedure, called contingent rechecking, could affect the rate of correct answers on daily math assignments (Cipani & McLaughlin, 1983). A 16-year-old student attending an educational treatment facility for students with emotional disturbances served as the participant. Math assignments were derived from three objectives. Each day, 10 items from each objective were selected from a pool of items and used as the measure of assignment accuracy.

The baseline condition involved the student finishing the assignment and turning it in. The teacher would then correct the assignment, report to the student how many errors were made, and ask her to try harder the next day. The range of percentage of correct answers during the baseline period was 57%–100%, with a mean of 79%.

The next condition was an office assistant reward with contingent rechecking. If the student earned at least a 95% correct grade when the assignment was turned in, she earned the privilege of being an office assistant for 45 minutes, twice a week. If she did not score at the 95% level, the teacher noted which problems were incorrect on a separate sheet of paper. The student was just told how many errors she had made and would have to go find them. She was not told which problems to fix. She then had to turn in her second attempt and hopefully catch all the errors to earn the privilege. The range of percentage correct on the first attempt during this condition was between 90%–100%, with a mean of 97%.

Condition C just involved the rechecking procedure. The follow-up phase involved the dropping of the contingent rechecking procedure (she was told she was doing well). Both conditions resulted in continued maintenance of results in the 90%–100% range.

## Research Example: Underachieving Students

An ambitious study selected 25 underachieving students from three school districts to determine whether social reinforcement and points could have an effect on classroom performance (Chadwick & Day, 1973). The participants in the study were 11 African American students and 14 Mexican American students. Their mean grade point average was 1.47 (out of 4). An experimental design was used to evaluate the effects of the following three conditions (ABC additive design): (1) baseline; (2) behavioral treatment package of earned points for backup reinforcers and teacher attention for appropriate behavior; and (3) removal of point contingency (i.e., just social attention provided).

Table 4.3 presents the data for each of the dependent variables. The means for each condition across percentage of on-task behavior are given in the second row. The next two rows depict the mean for each condition for rate of work completed and accuracy of work, respectively.

## Steps to Conducting Research Using Additive Designs

The steps to conducting single-case research using an additive design are given in Table 4.4.

## Advantages of Additive Designs

Additive designs provide the same practicality as AB designs for use in everyday classrooms. Teachers want to find something that addresses a problem they are experiencing. By following an ineffective treatment

### Table 4.3

**DATA FOR ON-TASK BEHAVIOR ACROSS AN ABC DESIGN**

| DEPENDENT VARIABLE | CONDITION | | |
| --- | --- | --- | --- |
| | BASELINE (A) | TREATMENT (B) | TREATMENT (C) (REMOVAL OF POINTS) |
| % on-task behavior | 39% | 57% | 42% |
| Rate of work completed (No. exercises completed) | 1.4 | 3.35 | 5.50 |
| Accuracy of work | 50% | 70% | 73% |

Table 4.4

**STEPS TO CONDUCTING RESEARCH USING AN ADDITIVE DESIGN**

1. Identify the dependent variable.
2. Define the dependent variable.
3. Design the observation system, including length of sessions and data collectors.
4. Graph data frequently (daily or at every session).
5. Implement the baseline condition until stability is achieved.
6. Implement the first treatment condition until stability is achieved.
7. In the absence of the desired effect, implement second treatment condition until data have stabilized within this condition.
8. Continue adding additional treatment conditions until the desired effect is achieved.

with other approaches, the additive design allows the teacher to try alternatives until some treatment or strategy is found that works. With a change in the behavior (dependent variable), the teacher solves the problem behavior. Like AB designs, additive designs can be used in situations where it may be necessary to prove that some procedure is effective.

For researchers in education, additive designs are useful in pilot work in attempting to uncover some possible treatment strategies that may look promising and can be further tested in a more rigorous experimental design.

## Limitations of Additive Designs

Additive designs are limited by the same factors that limit the AB design. The additive design does not demonstrate a cause-and-effect relationship between the treatment variables and behavior change, due to its failure to replicate the different experimental conditions and subsequently replicate the obtained effects. Additive designs further complicate the determination of cause and effect by the addition of extra conditions that may produce changes in behavior. The change in behavior depicted in Table 4.3 could be attributed either to the experimental condition or to sequence effects.

What are sequence effects? The effect obtained is more a function of the sequence of the condition than the actual treatment condition. Ms. Turner is interested in increasing the percentage of correct

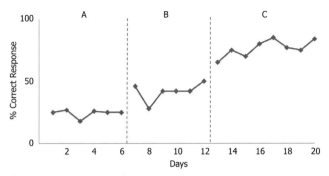

**Figure 4.5** Additive design illustrating three conditions.

responses given during oral reading lessons in her special day class. After a baseline condition (A), in which the rate of correct words read is simply recorded for each student who read a passage, she implements a praise condition (B). Each time a student reads three sentences correctly without an error, she will provide specific praise and reinforcement. Condition B is followed by Condition C, in which Ms. Turner has the students run outside for 20 minutes in the morning. The data in Figure 4.5 show that the rate of correct responses increases.

Can we conclude that Condition C is more effective than Condition B, given the significant change in mean and level of behavior? Sequence effects could be at work. Suppose the two treatment conditions were implemented in reverse order? In this case, treatment previously termed C would be implemented following the baseline, and then the treatment condition previously labeled B would be implemented last. If sequence effects are at work, we will see a better result with the C condition, whatever it is. The effect for any given treatment obtained depends on the sequence of conditions. Therefore, one is not justified in making cause-and-effect statements when using additive designs.

## REVERSAL DESIGNS

### Questions to Ponder

- How are reversal designs different from AB designs?
- How do they demonstrate experimental control of the independent variable?
- When would a researcher want to start with treatment (B) before beginning baseline (A), as in the case of a BABAB design?

- What is meant by the phrase "turning the behavior on and off"?
- What can be concluded when the behavior does not return to the baseline level upon activating the reversal condition?
- Are there any conditions that would limit the use of a reversal design?

## Brief Description of Reversal Designs

AB and additive designs do not demonstrate experimental control, and therefore they preclude any cause-and-effect conclusions. The potential for alternative explanations of what caused the change in behavior is inherent in those designs. However, other single-case designs can demonstrate experimental control by replicating one or more of the experimental conditions. The replication of previous conditions must be followed by the same level of behavior produced in these previous condition(s). AB or additive designs can be extended to include a replication of one or more of the experimental conditions to allow for this. Extending the data collection in an AB study to replicate the two experimental conditions produces an ABAB design. The replication of both the A and B condition extend the study to four phases.

Designs that replicate previous conditions are termed reversal designs. There are various types of reversal designs, of which some replicate just the baseline condition (termed ABA), others replicate just one treatment condition (termed BAB), while another replicates both baseline and treatment conditions (ABAB). The ABAB design involves replicating both the baseline and treatment conditions. It is a classic demonstration of experimental control of the independent variable. The ability to significantly change the level of behavior by changing the experimental condition has been termed "turning the behavior on and off" (Baer, Wolf, & Risley, 1968).

The BAB design is depicted in Figure 4.6. It involves the replication of a treatment condition, with a baseline condition between the two treatment conditions. This design starts with treatment (sometimes people are in a hurry to get something going). Following a treatment condition, a baseline is instituted, involving a removal of the treatment. If the behavior changes during the baseline period, the prior treatment is then reinstituted. This experimental manipulation results in a BAB design, that is, with a baseline sandwiched in between the treatments. The reintroduction of the original treatment condition results in the return of high levels of appropriate behavior (see Figure 4.6).

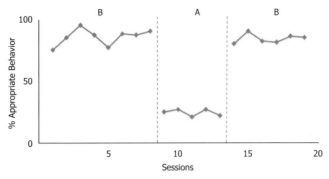

**Figure 4.6** BAB design.

## Examples of Reversal Designs

### An ABAB Design for Lunch Line Behavior

In a hypothetical example, a junior high school lunchroom supervisor is interested in changing the behavior of three students when they are in the lunch line. These three students come into the lunchroom together and seem to exacerbate each others' inappropriate behavior. Often they do not wait in line but try to cut in front of other students. They also engage in other inappropriate behaviors. The supervisor decides to define cafeteria rule violations as the following: cutting in front of other students in the line, bumping other students while in line, intentionally coughing on peers, and making taunting comments. A graduate student doing a thesis decides to select this problem as a topic for a research project. After clearing the proposal with her committee, she sets out to begin the data collection for her study. She measures the frequency of occurrence of the behaviors during the lunch period for all three students. She collects baseline data on the rate of rule violations across all three students and graphs them collectively (see Figure 4.7).

Following 10 days of baseline data collection, she implements a treatment program that incorporates positive consequences for not engaging in any of the designated rule violations. If the three students have a 0 rate of inappropriate rule violations, all three students get 10 points. If they engage in 1–3 incidents, they earn 7 points, and 4–6 incidents result in just 4 points. If they have more than 7 occurrences collectively, they get no points. Therefore, they can earn 4–10 points each lunch period to use for a weekly reinforcer, that is, a special activity in their classroom. This experimental condition is implemented for an 11-day period. Following this treatment condition period, the researcher returns to the

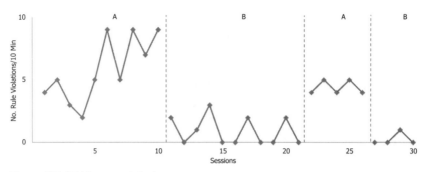

**Figure 4.7** ABAB reversal design.

baseline condition for 5 days and then returns to the treatment condition. The four phases comprise the ABAB design (see Figure 4.7).

Figure 4.7 shows that both the baseline condition and the treatment condition have been replicated. The phrase "turning the behavior on and off" is illustrated in an exemplary fashion in Figure 4.7. Note that a change in the level of behavior occurs with each change in condition. The first baseline period results in high rates of inappropriate behavior. Implementation of the treatment turns off the high level. Instituting the reversal turns the high level back on. The return to treatment turns the heightened level of behavior off again.

How do the data in Figure 4.7 demonstrate experimental control? Experimental control is demonstrated in reversal designs by the replication of one or more experimental conditions and the subsequent replication of similar effects obtained with the implementation of the same condition(s). The data depicted in Figures 4.6 and 4.7 demonstrate this. When baseline conditions are in effect, you see one level of behavior. When treatment conditions are in effect, you see a different level, irrespective of which phase you are examining.

In order to demonstrate experimental control in reversal designs, two things must occur. First, the replication of the experimental conditions must involve the exact same treatment, and baseline procedures must be replicated. In the example presented above, it would be erroneous to implement the group point system following the first baseline condition and then a completely different strategy after the second baseline condition has been implemented. Instead of an ABAB reversal design, one then has just two AB designs, with their inherent problems in demonstrating experimental control. Providing there is at least one previous condition replicated, experimental control of possible sources of error can be inferred. Second, the effects obtained under baseline conditions must be similar (and the same applies to the treatment condition).

## Research Example: 7-Year-Old Student

A research study used an ABAB design to determine the effectiveness of a treatment for a student's lack of compliance with teacher instructions (Belfiore, Basile, & Lee, 2008). This study is an excellent example of behavior analytic action research (Belfiore, Lee, Scheeler, & Klein, 2002). The student was a 7-year-old boy with Down syndrome, functioning in the moderate range of mental retardation and diagnosed with ADHD. The teacher often had to physically prompt him (i.e., hand over hand) to respond to many classroom requests. The student, Jeff, was enrolled in a life skills class with other children with developmental disabilities. Ten target commands resulted in low rates of compliance, for example, get your work, go to your desk. The student's compliance with these requests, issued in two daily sessions, constituted the dependent variable. During periods of the baseline condition, the commands were simply issued and data were collected on whether compliance with each of the 10 commands occurred. In the treatment condition, a high probability command sequence (HPCS) was issued before each target command. During the first baseline period, the percentage of compliance across seven sessions was 30%, 20%, 0%, 10%, 0%, 10%, and 10%. During the treatment, the following compliance percentage was obtained for the same commands: 80%, 90%, 70%, 70%, and 90%. The return to the baseline condition resulted in a drop in compliance to below 30% (rates similar to those obtained in the first baseline period). Reinstituting the HPCS treatment resulted in a return to good levels of compliance (above 80% for all data points). Experimental control was demonstrated by the researchers' ability to turn the behavior on and off. If there was any possibility that the change in behavior could be attributed to a variable other than the HPCS treatment, the data obtained from the return to baseline reduced such concerns.

## Research Example: Disruptive Hallway Behavior

An ABACBC design was used to evaluate the effects of public posting on disruptive hallway behavior during class changes involving 250 students in a junior high school (Staub, 1990). The dependent variable, disruptive behavior, involved such observable behaviors as hitting, pushing, or kicking others, running in the hallways, and using foul language (directed at someone or not). Following a baseline condition (Phase A), public posting was instituted (Phase B). Several signs in the hallways delineated the target disruptive behaviors. Following the public posting condition (B), a return to baseline was instituted (A). The next treatment condition (C) continued the public posting, with the addition of verbal feedback and praise for appropriate behavior (Phase C). Verbal feedback and praise consisted of statements made by the dean over the intercom, delineating the improvement in student behavior in the hallways, for example, "Great job, students, you have improved 10% from yesterday." To ensure experimental control, a return to Phase B was instituted followed by another installment of Phase C. The change in disruptive behavior from the initial baseline to the first public posting condition was from 63% to 43%. With the return to baseline, the rate of disruptive behavior rose to 49%. When verbal feedback and praise were added (C condition), the rate of disruptive behavior was reduced to 26%. The return of the public posting in the second B condition resulted in a higher rate of disruptive behavior (46%). The final C condition produced a decrease in the rate again. Additionally, the rate of detentions showed the same effect from these experimental conditions. The lowest rate of detentions was produced when the combined package was in effect.

## Research Example: Fourth-Grade Class

A study conducted in a fourth-grade class in California evaluated the relative effectiveness of two procedures designed to keep students' attention on lesson presentation (Christie & Schuster, 2003). These researchers compared hand raising (HR) with response cards (RC) as methods for enhancing student engagement. The class had 24 students enrolled, with diverse ethnic backgrounds. The school's overall standardized test score on the California Test of Basic Skills (CTBS), 44.8, was below the state mean of 52.5. An ABA design was used, with the RC condition (B) in between two HR conditions (A).

Math instruction occurred between 10:00 and 11:00 in the morning, with several instructional activities planned during that time, such as homework review, timed trials using a sheet of math problems, the presentation of new material, and guided practice with new material. It was during these latter two instructional activities that the HR and RC conditions were deployed.

In the HR condition, the students would raise their hands in response to teacher questions. The teacher would then call on one of them to answer, indicate whether the answer was right or wrong, and then proceed with more instruction or ask another question. In the RC condition, the teacher followed the same routine except that when she asked a question, all the members of the class wrote their answers on the response cards. The students then showed the teacher their answers by holding up their response cards on a signal.

Two student measures were taken: (1) on-task behavior; and (2) grades for daily quizzes on the covered material. Observers recorded on-task behavior for five target children whom the teacher considered to be representative of the class. Both of the measures were taken during the HR condition and the RC condition each day.

The results obtained showed the superiority of the RC procedure for some students who were having problems attending under the HR condition. As an illustration of the effect, Brad did not raise his hand once in the HR condition. In contrast, across five RC sessions, he wrote on his board an average of 97% of the total opportunities (i.e., responses to teacher questions). His mean daily quiz grade was 63% during HR as against 93% during RC. Similarly his on-task percentage was improved significantly, from a mean of 12.5% during HR to 100% during RC.

Some additional research studies using reversal designs are delineated in Table 4.5.

## Steps to Conducting Research Using ABAB Designs

Reversal designs require a replication of one or more experimental conditions. Therefore, the procedures vary slightly depending on whether the design is ABAB, BAB, ABCBC, or other. Table 4.6 presents the steps to conducting research using a reversal design in general.

## Advantages of Reversal Designs

The primary advantage of a reversal design is the ability to infer a cause-and-effect relationship. How does a reversal design allow for causal inferences? The possibility of bias effects from confounding variables can be ruled out when conditions are replicated across time and the same level of behavior change is obtained at each point in time. Confounding variables produce bias effects. Confounding variables are variables other

Table 4.5

**ADDITIONAL RESEARCH STUDIES USING A REVERSAL DESIGN**

| REFERENCE | REVERSAL DESIGN USED | DEPENDENT VARIABLE | EXPERIMENTAL CONDITIONS |
|---|---|---|---|
| ■ Hall, 1971 | ■ ABAB | ■ No. disputes (EXP 1) <br> ■ No. talk-outs (EXP 2) | ■ Baseline (A) <br> ■ Contingent attention for production (B) |
| ■ Lau & Cipani, 1983 | ■ BCACB | ■ Food waste (plate void of any amount of food before dessert) | ■ Individual point contingency (B) vs. group point contingency (C) vs. baseline (A) |
| ■ Trice & Parker, 1983 | ■ ABACA 1 child <br> ■ ACABC 2nd child | ■ Swearing in regular class, four students | ■ Baseline (A) <br> ■ Response cost (B) <br> ■ DRL (C) |
| ■ Austin & Agar, 2005 | ■ ABAB | ■ % compliance with task requests | ■ Baseline (A) <br> ■ HPCS (high probability command sequence) (B) |
| ■ Wilder, Harris, Reagan, & Rasey, 2007 | ■ ABAB | ■ % noncompliance | ■ Baseline (A) <br> ■ DRA (B) |

Table 4.6

**STEPS TO CONDUCTING RESEARCH USING AN ABAB DESIGN**

1. Identify the dependent variable.
2. Define the dependent variable.
3. Design the observation system, including length of sessions and data collectors.
4. Graph data frequently (daily or at every session).
5. Implement the baseline condition until stability is achieved.
6. Implement the treatment condition until stability is achieved.
7. Replicate the baseline condition by removing treatment and continue until data have stabilized within the reversal condition.
8. Replicate the treatment condition(s).

than the independent variable that may have changed at the same point in the study as the independent variable has.

A graphic illustration can be used to demonstrate the possibility of confounding variables and their effects. In examining hypothetical data on the rate of out-of-seat behavior in a first-grade class, examine the first AB conditions in Figure 4.8. Following a baseline period, during which the rate of out-of-seat occurrences was higher than seven for all but 1 week, the teacher implements a reprimand condition for out-of-seat behavior. The result of 5 weeks of data collection is a stable lower rate of out-of-seat occurrences. Within this 5-week period, all but 1 day was under three occurrences.

The teacher would like to conclude that the change in the students' behavior was the result of verbal reprimands for such behavior. However, it is possible that a host of other events could have occurred concurrently with the use of verbal reprimands. If this is so, one would expect that if the researcher returns to the verbal reprimand condition at a different time in the future, the same level of behavior may not result. The ABAB design in Figure 4.8 demonstrates what the data might look like if a variable other than the independent variable produced the behavior change.

The change evidenced in the first reprimand treatment condition was not replicated when this condition was replicated 10 weeks later (see verbal reprimand treatment condition data set). The second verbal reprimand condition failed to show any change, in the number of out-of-seat behaviors across the entire class, from the second baseline condition (see Figure 4.8). It would be plausible to assume that the behavior change that occurred in the first verbal reprimand treatment condition did not represent a change resulting from the independent variable (i.e., change from baseline condition to verbal

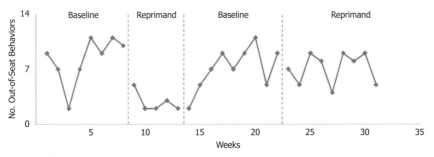

**Figure 4.8** Failure to demonstrate experimental control in an ABAB design.

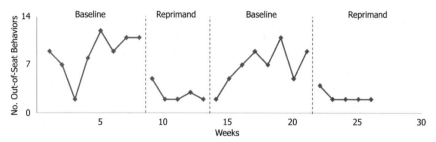

**Figure 4.9** Illustration of a cause-and-effect relationship between treatment condition and behavior.

reprimand procedure). This data set is illustrative of lack of experimental control.

The types of variables that might produce systematic bias effects on the data in an AB design might be passage of time, expectancy, change in periodic schedules, and similar events. The ABAB design allows the researcher or evaluator to rule out speculation about change in behavior due to these confounding variables. The reversal design achieves this ability by replicating the change in behavior with the change in conditions. If the data obtained in the study discussed above looked like those in Figure 4.9, a cause-and-effect relationship could be concluded. Note that the change in condition brings about a change in the mean frequency and level of behavior, each and every time!

## Limitations of Reversal Designs

The reversal design has three limitations relating to the reversal of effects issue.

### Failure to Replicate Prior Level of Behavior

The first limitation of the reversal design is that a failure to replicate the same level of behavior with the replication of the same experimental conditions makes the results ambiguous (as in the case of Figure 4.8). In Figure 4.8, the failure to replicate the same treatment effect for the second B (reprimand) condition makes any judgment about the efficacy of reprimands ambiguous. It is certainly unclear whether the change in the first treatment condition was caused by the teacher's use of the reprimand strategy or by something else, which may have coincided with the implementation of the treatment at that time.

## Ethical Issues

The second limitation of the reversal design is that the reversion of certain types of behaviors to baseline levels of could cause potential harm to the clients themselves or to others. It may be unethical to allow a return to high problematic levels of behavior due to the great potential for harm that accompanies behavior such as self-abuse, aggressive and/or violent behavior, running away from school grounds, and pica (ingestion of inedible objects). When the social and physical welfare of children might be jeopardized, one should consider another design for a study of these types of behaviors. For example, using a reversal design to evaluate a treatment strategy that produces a desirable change in aggressive behavior of junior high students in the first B (treatment) condition would be unethical. It is unjustifiable to go back to baseline levels to prove a point about experimental control when this will probably result in an increase in aggressive behavior.

## Nonreversible Effects

The third limitation is that some behaviors may not be reversible and therefore may not be amenable to a reversal design. Reversibility refers to the ability of the behavior to change in rate when conditions are changed. Acquisition behaviors (in contrast to change of rate behaviors) are responses that the client does not presently have in his or her repertoire. But once learned, they cannot be unlearned! For example, many motor skills (e.g., riding a bicycle, swimming, learning to multiply single-digit numbers, feeding oneself independently, etc.) will not reverse once they have been learned and therefore will not show low levels of acquisition when the baseline condition is reinstituted. There are also other behaviors, besides acquisition behaviors, that may not be reversible, due to the potency of existing natural reinforcers.

In summary, the reversal design, by replicating one or more experimental conditions and producing the same levels of behavior in these conditions as seen previously, allows causal inferences to be made regarding the independent variable. The same treatment condition must be replicated in the reversal design. Reversal designs require that effects be replicated for experimental control. Reversal designs may not be applicable when it is unethical to reverse a successful treatment and produce high levels of potentially dangerous behavior or when acquisition behaviors are being examined. Although reversal designs are well suited for applied research needs, the necessity to reverse an effective treatment might not be well suited to evaluation needs when such a reversal would be unethical.

## MULTIPLE BASELINE DESIGNS

### Questions to Ponder
- How is a multiple baseline design different from a reversal design?
- How does a multiple baseline design allow for a demonstration of experimental control?
- What are some considerations in selecting the type of multiple baseline designs you should use in your study?
- Are there any conditions that would limit the use of the multiple baseline design?

## Brief Description of Multiple Baseline Designs

In the previous section, you learned that a reversal design provides for an analysis of the effects of the treatment program on the student behavior (the dependent variable). However, due to the limitations of the reversal design, there exists a need for a different research design to demonstrate cause and effect in school settings. An alternative design that lessens these limitations is the multiple baseline design. The multiple baseline design involves applying the treatment condition to two or more baselines in a time-staggered fashion. This means that the treatment condition is implemented across different baseline measurements but at different times during the research study. The multiple baseline design can be likened to a number of AB designs with the baseline conditions being extended in length for each succeeding baseline (Hersen & Barlow, 1976). However, the data are collected on each baseline condition in the same time period. This excludes the collection of baseline and treatment condition data for one component and later collecting baseline and treatment condition data for another component (an exception to this is the multiple probe design).

## Examples of Multiple Baseline Designs

### Hypothetical Example of a Multiple Baseline Design

In a 10th-grade class, a science teacher has difficulty getting students in the third period to follow several class rules. She identifies two major problems during her class presentations: (1) inappropriate outbursts, and (2) use of personal items (e.g., text messaging on cell phones) during her lecture. She wants to target both of these behaviors to decrease their frequency. To demonstrate that the treatment intervention selected to address these two behaviors actually causes the decrease in such problem behaviors, she is implementing the intervention in a time-staggered approach across two baselines. The teacher will assess the effectiveness of a class-wide intervention, the Good Behavior Board Game (or GBBG), which uses a board game to increase adherence to class rules and reduce disruptive behavior (Cipani, 2008). First the Good Behavior Board Game will be applied just to the incidents of using a cell phone during class (including both sending and receiving). Once stability of data is achieved, she will then add to the Good Behavior Board Game the display of outbursts as a second target behavior.

Figure 4.10 displays the effects of the Good Behavior Board Game on the rates of the two problem behaviors. The baseline data collected simultaneously for both target behaviors show a high rate of both of these behaviors. At Session 6, the experimental condition (Good Behavior Board Game) is implemented but applied only to incidents involving cell phone use. In that manner, the second behavior (outbursts) serves as the control condition. As you can see, the incidents of this behavior decrease in Sessions 6–9. In contrast, the number of outbursts remains unaffected

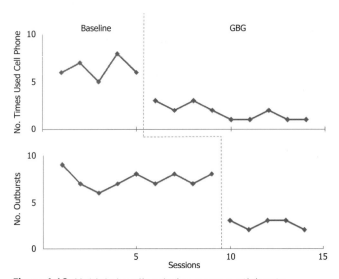

**Figure 4.10** Multiple baseline design across participants.

during this same time period. In Session 10, the experimental condition is applied to outbursts as well. This illustrates the time-staggered nature of the multiple baseline design. Once this second behavior is added to the treatment strategy, it also decreases dramatically, during Sessions 10–14. Note that the effect of treatment occurred only after the treatment was applied to that particular baseline.

### Research Example: Math Performance

Researchers used a multiple baseline across participants design in a comparison of three strategies to increase math performance (Dunlap & Dunlap, 1989). Three students with learning disabilities, one in fifth grade and two in sixth grade, served as participants for this study. These students had demonstrated difficulty with the computational subtraction skill involving regrouping. The dependent variable was the percentage of responses correct on the worksheet of problems involving regrouping. One student was given worksheets including 10–20 problems, and the other two students' worksheets contained a fixed number of problems each day, 12 and 10 respectively.

In the baseline condition, the teacher would present didactic instruction on the concept of regrouping, followed by the worksheet. In the second baseline condition, two points for each correct answer to a problem (part of an already existing incentive system) were added to the didactic lecture. In the final phase, a self-instruction monitoring sheet was added. Each student was given an individualized checklist of steps to follow in performing the regrouping subtraction problems. Each student was taught how to use the checklist and monitor whether he or she performed each step in each problem. One student was given a self-monitoring checklist (see Table 4.7).

Table 4.7

**SELF-MONITORING CHECKLIST**

- Copied the problem down correctly
- Regrouped when I needed to (top number is bigger than bottom number)
- Borrowed correctly (number crossed out)
- Subtracted all numbers
- Subtracted correctly

For all three students, neither the didactic training alone nor the didactic training combined with points produced significant changes in the percentage of correct answers on the students' daily worksheets. The results demonstrated that the self-monitoring package produced demonstrable gains in percentage correct for two of the students over both of their baselines. The third student showed an initial effect with the points condition, but the effect then tapered off.

## Research Example: Question Asking

The multiple baseline design is well suited for research on the acquisition of new skills. Teaching a student a new skill will make it difficult to reverse the effects by returning to the baseline condition. The multiple baseline study described below sought to develop question-asking skills in students in a mainstream math class (Knapczak, 1989). A multiple baseline across participants design was used to evaluate the effectiveness of a treatment strategy. The objective of the study was to increase the frequency of question-asking behavior during math instruction of three students with mild disabilities. The treatment was time staggered across the three students. Following the collection of baseline data, in a multiple baseline fashion, the first student received the treatment. The other two students remained in baseline. Once treatment effects stabilized, the second student received treatment while the third student remained in baseline. Finally, all three students received treatment once the treatment effects for Students 1 and 2 stabilized.

The treatment was rather elaborate in its method for developing the skill. Question asking is a verbal behavior that occurs when a student fails to comprehend the lesson presentation of the general education teacher. To teach such students to identify when they did not understand, the teacher was videotaped for three lessons. Each student and special education teacher viewed the tape together. The student was then prompted to identify if he or she understood the presentation or needed to ask a question. Additionally, the appropriate context for asking questions was taught: (1) ask questions during a break in the instructional activity; or (2) ask questions when the teacher prompts the class for questions. As a result of the training, there was a significant increase in question asking for all three students. This effect only occurred once the students received the training. Additionally, the percentage of accuracy on assigned seat work showed a substantial increase following treatment.

*Research Example: Low Performers*

A study that evaluated the effects of an instructional package and peer tutoring on low-performing first-grade students' competence in using a number line succeeded in its aims (Fueyo & Bushell, 1998). Three groups with three students in each group served as participants for a peer tutoring package. These students demonstrated on a pretest little or no skill in using a number line to find a missing addend. An instructional package involving 14 steps was developed and used by the three peer tutors (one tutor per group). When this training was given with feedback on the accuracy of the students' performance, all three groups in using the number line for basic computations increased. This study was novel in that all three groups were also compared to a no-tutoring control group, in which the skill of the three students involved did not improve.

*Research Example: Multiplication Facts*

A multiple baseline design across five different behaviors (types of multiplication fact) was used to evaluate an instructional package on the rate of acquisition of correct multiplication facts (Wood, Frank, & Wacker, 1998). Three students with learning disabilities served as participants in the study. Two of the students were in a third-grade class during math instruction, where multiplication facts were targeted for acquisition. The third participant was a fifth-grade student who had not yet acquired multiplication fact skills. Using the multiple baseline design across behaviors, the researchers were able to demonstrate that the effects on the group occurred only at the point at which the instructional package was implemented for the group.

Some additional research studies using multiple baseline designs are delineated in Table 4.8.

## Steps to Conducting Research Using Multiple Baseline Designs

Multiple baseline designs require a staggered approach to implementing the treatment or intervention. There are several types of multiple baseline designs that stagger treatment across different participants, settings, or behaviors. The procedures vary only slightly, depending on the specific design being utilized. Table 4.9 presents the steps to conducting research using a multiple baseline design in general.

Table 4.8

### ADDITIONAL RESEARCH STUDIES USING MULTIPLE BASELINE DESIGNS

| REFERENCE | MULTIPLE BASELINE DESIGN (MBD) USED | DEPENDENT VARIABLE(S) | EXPERIMENTAL CONDITIONS |
|---|---|---|---|
| ■ Barbetta & Miller, 1991 | ■ Multiple probe baseline designs across behaviors (sets of words) | ■ Number of sight vocabulary words read correctly, words read in sentences correctly, other | ■ Baseline vs. Tugmate (A cross-age tutoring program) with six 1st–3rd graders |
| ■ Pratt-Struthers, Struthers, & Williams, 1983 | ■ MBD across behaviors (groups of target words) | ■ % target words spelled correctly in creative writing | ■ Baseline vs. Add-A-Word program |
| ■ Hughes & Hendrickson, 1987 | ■ MBD across three groups of at-risk students | ■ % on-task behavior | ■ Baseline vs. self-monitoring |
| ■ Brown, Copeland, & Hall, 1986 | ■ MBD across three grade levels (307 students) | ■ No. correct multiplication facts | ■ Baseline vs. group feedback vs. Group & individual feedback vs. other conditions |
| ■ Nelson, Alber, & Gordy, 2004 | ■ MBD across students | ■ No. words read correctly/minute | ■ Baseline vs. Error correct (EC) vs. EC & repeated reading (RR) vs. EC & RR & prior |

## Advantages of Multiple Baseline Designs

The multiple baseline design provides the researcher with the ability to demonstrate experimental control over the independent variable. By producing the change in behavior *at the point* when the treatment is applied to each baseline leg, it allows one to determine cause and effect between treatment and change in behavior. By staggering the treatment, it enables the unaffected baselines to serve as the control condition. This allows the researcher to rule out any confounding variables as a possible explanation of the effects on the treated baselines.

The multiple baseline design also avoids the pitfalls of reversal designs, by not requiring a return to baseline. In the example given above, a study of the effects of a treatment program on aggressive behavior, the teacher or researcher would just have to collect several baselines. If the treatment

Table 4.9

---

**STEPS TO CONDUCTING RESEARCH USING A MULTIPLE BASELINE DESIGN**

1. Identify the dependent variable.
2. Define the dependent variable.
3. Design the observation system, including length of sessions and data collectors.
4. Graph data frequently (daily or at every session).
5. Determine whether the baselines that will be collected will be across different participants (MBD across participants), across different settings with the same participant (MBD across settings), or across different behaviors within same participant (MBD across behaviors).
6. Implement the baseline condition until stability is achieved.
7. Implement the treatment condition with the first leg only until stability is achieved, while other baselines remain in baseline condition.
8. Stagger intervention across the other baselines in the same fashion.

---

program reduces the rate of aggressive behavior significantly without any serious side effects, then it can be systematically applied to the other baselines, in a time-staggered fashion. It therefore avoids the ethical dilemma, since there is no need to return to baseline. Hence a probable increase in aggressive behavior with such a return does not have to occur.

## Limitations of Multiple Baseline Designs

### More Work

One limitation of the multiple baseline design is that the researcher must collect data on additional behaviors, settings, or participants. However, the ability of the multiple baseline design to experimentally control the independent variable without a reversal condition makes it attractive in spite of the additional data collection required.

### Point of Effect

A more significant limitation is that the experimental effects have to occur only at the point where the treatment condition is implemented for each component. The multiple baseline design demonstrates experimental control of the independent variable by generating an effect for each component (or baseline) only at the point where the intervention is applied, and not before. Changes in the behavior of components that have not received the treatment procedure make conclusions regarding experimental effects ambiguous. Experimental control is demonstrated by producing a change in the behavior(s) not currently under the treatment condition. Let's illustrate this by utilizing the effects of the Good Behavior Board Game (see Figure 4.11) on two target behaviors in 10th-grade science class.

The graph in Figure 4.11 demonstrates a change in the frequency of inappropriate cell phone use with the implementation of the Good Behavior Board Game. However, at the same time, the frequency of outbursts also decreases (examine Sessions 6–9 and contrast with Sessions 1–5), without treatment being applied to this behavior. The baseline that was designated as the control condition evidences a change as well. The set of data in Figure 4.11 does not provide clear evidence that a functional relationship exists between change in behavior and the presence or absence of the treatment procedure.

If change is seen in a component still in the baseline (control) condition, it is uncertain as to whether this change is due to generalized (or carryover) effects or to a confounding variable. Generalized effects are the result of the spreading of the treatment effects to untreated behaviors. This is seen as a positive side effect of the treatment (changes in other behaviors not targeted for intervention at that time). Confounding variables produce a change in behavior due to uncontrolled variables

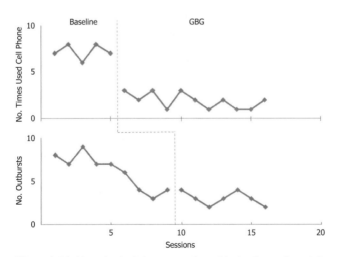

**Figure 4.11** Hypothetical demonstration of lack of experimental control in a multiple baseline design.

(time, maturation, sensitization to a treatment). These are undesirable and do not point to the efficacy of the treatment condition. Looking at the data presented in Figure 4.11, one cannot determine whether the changes in the untreated baseline in Sessions 6–9 are the result of generalized effects or confounding variables.

One proposed solution to the problem of finding out which effects are occurring is to collect data on three more components (baselines). The investigator should try at least to select three behaviors that are topographically distinct, so that changes in one behavior (as a function of the treatment procedure) will not generalize to the other two behaviors. A second solution to this problem is to implement a reversal condition in one or more of the components. The best way to accomplish this would be to implement the reversal conditions initially in the first leg of the multiple baseline and demonstrate experimental control before proceeding further in applying consequences to other components. Of course, the inherent problem with this solution is the limitations incurred by a reversal condition, explicated above.

## Types of Multiple Baseline Designs

There are three major types of multiple baseline designs: (1) multiple baseline across different participants, (2) multiple baseline across different settings, and (3) multiple baseline across different behaviors. All three types utilize the time-staggered approach in introducing the treatment condition to each component. However, the difference is in selecting either multiple behaviors (in the same participant and setting), multiple participants (with the same target behavior and the same setting), or multiple settings (same behaviors) and participant(s).

As Table 4.10a illustrates, the multiple baseline across participants design time staggers the treatment across three different individual participants. The setting is usually the same (e.g., the classroom) and the target behavior is the same for all three participants. In Phase 1 of the study, every participant is in the baseline condition. In Phase 2, only the first participant receives the treatment. The other two participants remain in the baseline condition, which thereby serves as the control condition. In Phase 3 of the study, the treatment is extended to the second participant, with the first participant continuing to receive treatment. The third participant is still in the baseline condition, which serves as the control condition. Finally, in Phase 4 of the study, all participants are receiving treatment.

The multiple baseline across different settings design time staggers the intervention across different baselines from various settings. As Table 4.10b illustrates, the multiple baseline design across settings time staggers the treatment across different settings for the same participant. Furthermore, the target behavior is the same for all three settings. If more than one participant is to take part in the study, there will be three multiple baseline designs, that is, one for each participant.

In Phase 1 of the study (see Table 4.10b), all three settings are in the baseline condition. In Phase 2, only the first setting (i.e., the classroom) receives treatment. The other two baselines continue and remain as the control conditions. The treatment is extended to the second setting (play area) in Phase 3, while the third setting (hallways) serves as the control condition. Finally, in Phase 4 of the study, all settings are exposed to the treatment. The same logic applies to the multiple baseline across behaviors design (see Table 4.11).

As Table 4.11 illustrates, the multiple baseline across different behaviors design time staggers the treatment across each of the three

## Table 4.10a

### MULTIPLE BASELINE DESIGN ACROSS DIFFERENT PARTICIPANTS

| PARTICIPANT | PHASE 1 | PHASE 2 | PHASE 3 | PHASE 4 |
|---|---|---|---|---|
| ■ 1 | ■ Baseline | ■ Treatment | ■ Treatment | ■ Treatment |
| ■ 2 | ■ Baseline | ■ Baseline | ■ Treatment | ■ Treatment |
| ■ 3 | ■ Baseline | ■ Baseline | ■ Baseline | ■ Treatment |

## Table 4.10b

### MULTIPLE BASELINE DESIGN ACROSS DIFFERENT SETTINGS

| PARTICIPANT | PHASE 1 | PHASE 2 | PHASE 3 | PHASE 4 |
|---|---|---|---|---|
| ■ Setting 1 (classroom) | ■ Baseline | ■ Treatment | ■ Treatment | ■ Treatment |
| ■ Setting 2 (play area) | ■ Baseline | ■ Baseline | ■ Treatment | ■ Treatment |
| ■ Setting 3 (hallways) | ■ Baseline | ■ Baseline | ■ Baseline | ■ Treatment |

Table 4.11

| MULTIPLE BASELINE DESIGN ACROSS DIFFERENT BEHAVIORS | | | | |
| --- | --- | --- | --- | --- |
| **PARTICIPANT** | **PHASE 1** | **PHASE 2** | **PHASE 3** | **PHASE 4** |
| ■ Behavior 1 | ■ Baseline | ■ Treatment | ■ Treatment | ■ Treatment |
| ■ Behavior 2 | ■ Baseline | ■ Baseline | ■ Treatment | ■ Treatment |
| ■ Behavior 3 | ■ Baseline | ■ Baseline | ■ Baseline | ■ Treatment |

behaviors. The setting is usually the same (e.g., the classroom) and the data is displayed for each individual participant. Note that treatment is extended systematically across each baseline in the time-staggered fashion. Finally, in the fourth phase of the study, all behaviors are subjected to the treatment condition.

## Summary

In summary, the multiple baseline design does not have to implement a reversal condition but rather time-staggers the treatment condition along multiple components to demonstrate experimental control of the independent variable. Experimental control of the treatment effect is demonstrated by the production of changes in behavior at the point where the intervention is initiated for each component. Changes that occur in a component still in the baseline condition following the introduction of the treatment condition to one component could be due either to generalized effects or to confounding variables. One method of discerning which variable is in effect is to collect data on three or more components. A second solution, in attempting to separate generalized effects from nonspecific effects, is to implement a reversal condition within the first component. The multiple baseline design, due to its ability to demonstrate the efficacy of the treatment condition as well as its lack of a reversal phase, is well suited for many applied research projects.

## MULTIELEMENT DESIGNS (aka ALTERNATING TREATMENTS DESIGNS)

### Questions to Ponder
- Why is it wise to include a baseline before, during, or even after a multielement analysis of three different treatments?

- How does multielement design allow for a cause-and-effect analysis?
- What are some concerns with regard to demonstrating experimental control with the multielement design?

## Brief Description of Multielement Designs

The multielement design involves the comparison of a number of different treatment and baseline conditions simultaneously. To achieve this, a quick switching of conditions is necessary. Switching conditions can be done every other session, every several sessions, or randomly. The multielement design can be likened to a reversal design utilizing a large number of reversals with just a few data points under each different condition. This design demonstrates experimental control by producing different rates of behavior under different conditions that are implemented at the same period of time. Figure 4.12 illustrates a hypothetical comparison of two treatment conditions with regard to on-task behavior: the beeper system[1] and an ignoring condition. These two conditions were alternated; one day the beeper system was in effect and the other day the ignoring condition was in effect.

The comparison between the beeper system and the ignoring condition with respect to on-task behavior illustrates the greater effectiveness of the beeper system (see Figure 4.13). The on-task rate of the class involved during the use of the beeper system was between 50% and 80%. The rate during the ignoring condition was between 7% and 30%. This reveals a clear distinction between the effects of the two conditions. Again, the multielement design must demonstrate the ability to turn behavior on and off for a clear demonstration of a functional relationship.

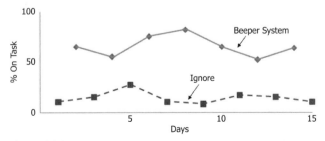

**Figure 4.12** Multielement design comparing the beeper system with an ignoring condition with on-task behavior.

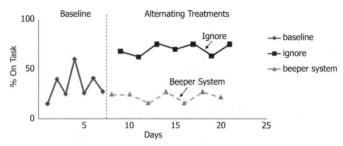

**Figure 4.13** Multielement design with initial baseline condition.

## Examples of Multielement Designs

### Research Example: Sight Word Reading

A multielement design was used to evaluate the effectiveness of two different error correction procedures with regard to the acquisition of sight words (Worsdell et al., 2005). In the first study, six persons with developmental disabilities underwent two error correction procedures after measurements were taken in a baseline condition. The baseline condition consisted of no correction provided by the teacher for reading errors. One of the treatment procedures involved providing an immediate single response correction for an error (single response or SR repetition). This required the participant to practice the correct pronunciation of the word once. The therapist would say, "This word is comb; say comb." This would be followed by the participant saying the modeled word once. In the second condition, called multiple response (MR) repetition, the participant had to repeat the correct pronunciation three times after each error.

Both error correction strategies were more effective than the baseline condition on the number of words mastered as well as the total number of correct responses. The MR condition was more effective eventually than the SR condition. As an example, Ernie, a participant in the study, mastered 70% more words in the MR condition than in the SR condition. Increased repetition was found to be more effective than single repetition of the correct response.

### Research Example: Bilingual Youth

An alternating treatments design was used in comparing two types of pre-instruction on the number of words read correctly during student oral reading by eight bilingual youths with speech impairments (Rousseau & Tam, 1991). The researchers selected this design since it did not require a reversal condition but rather would allow one of the two instructional procedures to be used in each reading session. The dependent variable was the number of words read correctly in a 1-minute timed passage from a story for beginning readers. The two treatments compared were listening/discussion and silent/discussion. In the former treatment, the teacher wrote approximately 10 key words on the board from the passage for that day. She then discussed the pronunciation and meaning of the words, and read the passage aloud for 5 minutes. She instructed the students to follow along while she read.

In the silent/discussion approach, the procedures were the same as in the listening/discussion treatment, except that the students did not hear the teacher read the passage but were just told to read silently and point to each word they read. The results demonstrated a higher percentage of words read correctly in the listening/discussion approach, when compared with the silent/discussion approach, for six of the eight students. This comparison reveals the superiority of the listening/discussion approach.

Some additional research studies using multiple-element designs are delineated in Table 4.12.

## Steps to Using a Multielement Design With an Initial Baseline

There are many variations of multielement designs. Table 4.13 provides a sequence for conducting research using a multielement design with an initial baseline.

Table 4.12

### ADDITIONAL RESEARCH STUDIES USING MULTIELEMENT DESIGNS

| REFERENCE | MULTIELEMENT DESIGN USED | DEPENDENT VARIABLE(S) | EXPERIMENTAL CONDITIONS |
|---|---|---|---|
| ■ Kodak, Northrup, & Kelley, 2007 | ■ One phase | ■ Problem behaviors/min for two students | ■ After a functional assessment, multiple treatments tested |
| ■ Potoczak, Carr, & Michael, 2007 | ■ Two phases | ■ % target behaviors | ■ Compared easy with difficult |

Table 4.13

| STEPS TO USING A MULTIELEMENT DESIGN WITH INITIAL BASELINE |
| --- |

1. Identify the dependent variable.
2. Define the dependent variable.
3. Design the observation system, including length of sessions and data collectors.
4. Graph data frequently (daily or at every session).
5. Implement the baseline condition until stability is achieved.
6. Implement alternating treatment conditions, by randomly assigning conditions to days, until stability is achieved for each condition.
7. If necessary, implement a second baseline condition.

## Advantages and Limitations of Multielement Designs

The multielement design is advantageous in that a number of experimental conditions can be compared in a much shorter time than is possible using other single-case designs. However, there are two limitations in using this design.

### Contrast Effects

The first limitation was alluded to earlier, that is, contrast effects. It is possible that in comparing certain experimental conditions within the same time frame, the effects obtained may be different from those that a reversal design would yield. This can happen when the effects of two reinforcers, for example, money versus praise, are compared on alternate days. The preferred reinforcer (money) makes the other reinforcer (praise) less appealing. Consequently, a lower level of performance is obtained in the praise condition when it is followed on the next day by a monetary contingency. If praise is alternated with a baseline condition, it will yield a substantially higher performance. Contrast effects serve to enlarge the magnitude of difference between experimental conditions due to the nature of the specific comparison being made.

### Carryover Effects

A second limitation is the possibility of carryover effects given the quick-switching nature of the multielement design. Carryover effects refer to one condition rubbing off on the other experimental condition. This can result in an inflation of the level of behavior under one condition due to the quick switch to the other, more powerful treatment condition. Carryover effects serve to decrease the difference between experimental conditions, particularly if the participant cannot discriminate as to when each contingency is in effect.

One factor that reduces the potential for carryover effects in multielement analyses is the fact that that the different experimental conditions are discriminable to the participant. With participants who can profit from cues and instructions on the experimental condition being implemented on that particular session/day, carryover would seem to be less likely. If this design is to be used, discriminable context change, signaling different contingencies or treatments, should be instituted. However, with some students, such as children with severe disabilities, verbal cues or other stimuli may fail to inform them of the change in contingencies. Hence, the probability of carryover effects would seem to be more likely with these students.

## Types of Multielement Designs

One type of multielement design is just alternating between treatment conditions. This can only work if one of the conditions produces a different noticeable effect from the effect produced by the other(s), as is the case in Figure 4.13. However, many researchers feel the need to collect baseline data prior to evaluating it in comparison with another condition (see Figure 4.13). This is done to decrease the chance of contrast effects that would enlarge the difference between the two conditions in a multielement analysis.

The difference in behavior between the two conditions might not be as great in a reversal design as would appear in a multielement analysis. Contrast effects will be discussed in more detail in a later section. However, collecting baseline data prior to the comparison of the two conditions would indicate whether the behavior in the baseline condition deteriorated as a result of being augmented by the reinforcement condition in the same period of time in the research study. Figure 4.13 indicates that this did not occur; the baseline data remained at about the same level throughout the entire data collection period.

A third type of multielement design that is advocated in preference to the previously discussed types is a design in which treatment conditions are tested simultaneously between two baseline conditions.

The implementation of the most effective treatment is initiated after the second baseline condition. Figure 4.14 shows a comparison of the effect on the rate of disruptive behavior of two different treatment conditions (reprimands and tokens), implemented after one baseline condition and before the other.

By utilizing this design, one can compare these two treatment procedures against baseline levels of responding. Since both procedures revealed a decrease in the rate of behavior, it is necessary to establish that this occurred as a result of the two treatments and not just as a result of a confounding variable such as sequence or time. Instituting another baseline condition after this multielement comparison, with the resulting increase in disruptive behavior, allows for an unambiguous conclusion regarding the effectiveness of the two treatment conditions. This data set demonstrates that the change in disruptive behavior in both procedures was a function of those conditions. This type of multielement design can be likened to an ABA reversal design. By implementing the baseline conditions in a time period other than within the multielement phase, one can compare a larger number of experimental conditions and get a more accurate level of baseline performance (by decreasing the chance of any carryover effects from an experimental condition to the baseline condition). Figure 4.14 shows that both treatment conditions produced lower levels of disruptive behavior than the baseline condition and that the reprimands condition was slightly more effective than the token condition in reducing this behavior. The more effective treatment can be reinstituted as a final condition, to reestablish an appropriate, desirable level of disruptive behavior.

In summary, the multielement design involves a quick switching of experimental conditions and demonstrates experimental control by pro-

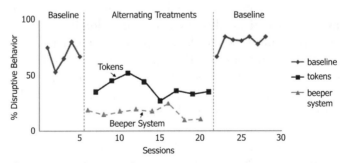

**Figure 4.14** Effect of tokens versus beeper system when compared to baseline condition.

ducing different rates of behavior under different conditions implemented in the same time period. While there are three variations of multielement designs, the type advocated is the implementation of a number of experimental (treatment) conditions within two baseline conditions, and the replication of the multielement analysis after the second baseline condition.

## CHANGING-CRITERION DESIGNS

### Questions to Ponder
- What types of research studies is a changing criterion design suited for?
- Does this design allow for a cause-and-effect analysis? What are some arguments for and against its suitability for a cause-and-effect analysis?
- What are some of the limitations of a changing criterion design?

## Brief Description of Changing Criterion Designs

The changing criterion design does what its name implies: It involves changing the criterion level at various stages of time during the study. A criterion level specifies a performance level to be achieved as a function of the training given. Once the behavior level reaches the first specified criterion level consistently, a new criterion level is established. This design can be used with acquisition behaviors that involve a number of component steps (e.g., learning how to brush teeth or wash hands independently, losing weight, etc.). This design also seems to be particularly applicable to behaviors involving small stepwise increases or decreases in rates of behavior. Figure 4.15 illustrates the changing criterion design, depicting the number of steps performed correctly with a junior high school special education student in a vocational-training class. The table-cleaning task has eight steps. The changing criterion design is deployed by setting the criterion number of steps in blocks of two, that is, first target goal is two correct steps, then four, and so forth. Each session, the teacher records how many steps the student performs correctly on her assigned table to clean. The teacher begins this training program by teaching the student the first two steps of this task on Monday. The criterion for this part of the changing criterion design is two steps correct. The teacher then records the number of steps the student performs correctly for the next six sessions. By the third session, the student is performing

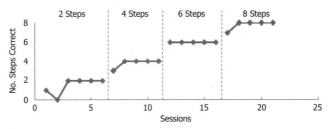

**Figure 4.15** Changing criterion design.

the two trained steps correctly but is not performing any of the other steps. Subsequently, prior to session 7, the teacher trains this student in the next two steps of this task and she quickly learns these as well. Sessions 8–11 show that this student is now performing four of the eight steps correctly. When the teacher trains the student to perform the next two steps correctly, she does so across the next five sessions, as well as correctly performing the prior four steps. Finally, with the last two steps of this task taught, the student performs all steps to mastery for the last five sessions. Figure 4.15 shows experimental control by producing changes in the behavior only at the point where the criterion is changed.

## Example of a Changing Criterion Design

A changing criterion design was used to demonstrate the effectiveness of a treatment program for an 11-year-old child with separation anxiety disorder (Flood & Wilder, 2004). Prior to treatment, the child would scream and plead anytime the mother left his area in the home. The dependent variable was a latency measure of this child's emotional behavior. This was quantified as the length of time that lapsed from when his mother left him to his crying. A baseline condition was followed by a treatment package. The treatment package involved a shaping program combined with the reinforcement of nonemotional behavior (i.e., not screaming or pleading) for a designated time interval. Treatment sessions were implemented twice per week in the home.

The shaping program manipulated two relevant variables: (1) the distance the mother was from the child, and (2) the length of time for which she would leave his immediate area. The treatment began reinforcing the child for not engaging in emotional behavior with access to a preferred play item when the mother was 10 feet away from him for 3 minutes. The treatment progressively altered the length of time in this variable in the following manner: from 3 minutes to 6, 12, 24, and 90 minutes.

The manner in which distance was progressively increased was from 10 feet to 20, 40, and 60 feet, followed by the mother leaving the premises.

The results demonstrated the utility of this treatment package with regard to emotional behavior. The mother was able to leave the premises for 90 minutes without the occurrence of any emotional behavior at the end of treatment.

## Steps to Conducting Research Using Changing Criterion Designs

Table 4.14 provides a sequence for conducting a changing criterion design.

## Advantages and Limitations of Changing Criterion Designs

The changing criterion design is well suited to studying instructional effects when the target skill is composed of a number of steps or phases. The steps should not provide for any spillover from treatment. One limitation of the design is that each criterion should be significantly different from the previous one, so as to allow for a visually apparent difference.

Table 4.14

### STEPS TO USING A CHANGING CRITERION DESIGN

1. Identify the dependent variable.
2. Define the dependent variable.
3. Design the observation system, including length of sessions and data collectors.
4. Graph data frequently (daily or at every session).
5. Designate a treatment strategy involving teaching procedures.
6. Designate the first level or standard.
7. Teach to that level or to component steps.
8. Designate the second level or standard.
9. Teach to that level or to component steps.
10. Data should indicate acquisition of skill to the designated number of steps.
11. Continue this process until the skill is acquired fully (all steps) or the highest standard is reached.

There must not be any trending in the data toward the next criterion, so as to allow for experimental control of the independent variable.

A related limitation is that the design does not totally eliminate other possible explanations of the change. It is acceptable to use a changing criterion design and demonstrate experimental control, given that the data does not trend toward the next criterion.

In summary, the changing criterion involves changing the criterion with subsequent changes in behavior to the level specified by the criterion only. If the changes in the condition vastly exceed those specified by the criterion, experimental control is not demonstrated. Two limitations are as follows: (1) each criterion has to be significantly different from the previous one to make the differences visually apparent, and (2) alternative explanations of the behavior change are plausible. The changing criterion design is well suited for studying acquisition behavior in research as well as evaluation projects.

## NOTE

1. For a complete description of the beeper system, see Cipani (2008).

## REFERENCES

Austin, J. L., & Agar, G. (2005). Helping young children follow their teachers' directions: The utility of high probability command sequences in pre-K and kindergarten classrooms. *Education and Treatment of Children, 28,* 222–236.

Baer, D. M., Wolf, M. M., & Risley, T. R. (1968). Some current dimensions of applied behavior analysis. *Journal of Applied Behavior Analysis, 1,* 91–97.

Barbetta, P. M., & Miller, A. D. (1991). Tugmate: A cross-age tutoring program to teach sight vocabulary. *Education and Treatment of Children, 14,* 19–38.

Belfiore, P. J., Basile, S. P., & Lee, D. L. (2008). Using a high probability command sequence to increase classroom compliance: The role of behavioral momentum. *Journal of Behavioral Education, 17,* 160–171.

Belfiore, P. J., Lee, D. L., Scheeler, M. C., & Klein, D. (2002). Implications of behavioral momentum and academic achievement for students with behavioral disorders: Linking theory with practice. *Psychology in the Schools, 39,* 171–180.

Brown, R. E., Copeland, R. E., & Hall, R. V. (1986). Effects of principal implemented procedures on student acquisition of multiplication facts. *Education and Treatment of Children, 9,* 202–220.

Chadwick, B. A., & Day, R. C. (1973). Systematic reinforcement: Academic performance of underachieving students. *Journal of Applied Behavior Analysis, 4,* 311–319.

Christie, C. A., & Schuster, J. W. (2003). The effects of using response cards on student participation, academic achievement, and on-task behavior during whole-class math instruction. *Journal of Behavioral Education, 12,* 147–165.

Cipani, E. (2008). *Classroom management for all teachers: Evidence-based plans.* Columbus, OH: Merrill/Prentice Hall.

Cipani, E., & McLaughlin, T. F. (1983). The use of contingent re-checking in modifying academic performance. *Corrective and Social Psychiatry, 29,* 88–93.

Dunlap, L. K., & Dunlap, G. (1989). A self-monitoring package for teaching subtraction with regrouping to students with learning disabilities. *Journal of Applied Behavior Analysis, 22,* 309–314.

Flood, W. A., & Wilder, D. A. (2004). The use of differential reinforcement and fading to increase time away from a caregiver in a child with separation anxiety disorder. *Education and Treatment of Children, 27,* 1–8.

Fueyo, V., & Bushell, D. (1998). Using number line procedures and peer tutoring to improve the mathematics computation of low-performing first graders. *Journal of Applied Behavior Analysis, 31,* 417–430.

Gosschalk, P. O. (2004). Behavioral treatment of acute onset school refusal in a 5-year-old girl with separation anxiety disorder. *Education and Treatment of Children, 27,* 150–160.

Hall, R. V., Fox, R., Willard, D., Goldsmith, L., Emerson, M., Owen, M., et al. (1971). The teacher as observer and experimenter in the modification of disputing and talk-out behaviors. *Jaba, 4,* 141–149.

Hersen, M., & Barlow, D. H. (1976). *Single-case experimental designs: Strategies in studying behavior change.* New York: Pergamon Press.

Hughes, C. A., & Hendrickson, J. M. (1987). Self-monitoring with at-risk students in the regular class. *Education and Treatment of Children, 10,* 225–236.

Knapczak, D. R. (1989). Generalization of student question asking from special class to regular class settings. *Journal of Applied Behavior Analysis, 22,* 77–83.

Kodak, T., Northrup, J., & Kelley, M. E. (2007). An evaluation of the types of attention that maintain problem behavior. *Journal of Applied Behavioral Analysis, 40,* 167–171.

Lau, W., & Cipani, E. (1983). Reducing student food waste in a cafeteria style dining setting through contingency management. *Child Care Quarterly, 12,* 301–310.

Nelson, J. S., Alber, S. R., & Gordy, A. (2007). Effects of systematic error correction and repeated readings on the reading accuracy and proficiency of second graders with disabilities. *Education and Treatment of Children, 27,* 186–198.

Potoczak, K., Carr, J. E., & Michael, J. (2007). The effects of consequence manipulation during functional analysis of problem behavior maintained by negative reinforcement. *Journal of Applied Behavior Analysis, 40,* 719–724.

Pratt-Struthers, J., Struthers, T. B., & Williams, R. L. (1983). The effects of the Add-A-Word Spelling Program on spelling accuracy during creative writing. *Education and Treatment of Children, 6,* 277–283.

Rousseau, M. K., & Tam, B. K. Y. (1991). The efficacy of previewing and discussion of key words on the oral reading proficiency of bilingual learners with speech and language impairments. *Education and Treatment of Children, 14,* 199–210.

Staub, R. W. (1990). The effects of publicly posted feedback on middle school students' disruptive behavior. *Education and Treatment of Children, 13,* 113–120.

Trice, A. D., & Parker, F. C. (1983). Decreasing student swearing in an instructional setting. *Education and Treatment of Children, 6,* 29–35.

Wilder, D. A., Harris, C., Reagan, R., & Ramsey, A. (2007). Functional analysis and treatment of noncompliance by preschool children. *Jaba, 40,* 173–177.

Wood, D. K., Frank, A. R., & Wacker, D. P. (1998). Teaching multiplication facts to students with learning disabilities. *Journal of Applied Behavior Analysis, 31,* 323–338.

Worsdell, A. S., Iwata, B. A., Dozier, C. L., Johnson, A. D., Neidert, P. L., & Thomason, J. L. (2005). Analysis of response repetition as an error-correction strategy during sight-word reading. *Journal of Applied Behavior Analysis, 38,* 511–527.

# 5

# Types of Single-Case Research Studies

## DECIDING ON THE TYPE OF RESEARCH STUDY

Very often, students have difficulty narrowing down their prospective research study. "I want to do something on the effects of computers on student learning." While this may seem like a laudable project, it does not provide enough of a focus. What dependent variable is of interest? Will it be a study that demonstrates how effectively a piece of instructional software can teach a specific targeted skill? Or will it compare computer-assisted instruction with a more traditional form of instruction on some measure of learning? What content area will be examined, for example, math, reading, science? What grade levels are of interest?

There are many aspects of classroom practice that are in need of empirical inquiry. For your thesis, you need to designate a research area or topic. You want to consider the feasibility of conducting such an applied research study. In some cases, the area of inquiry is dictated (to some degree) by the teaching position you hold (if applicable). Conducting research in your own classroom, once all the administrative and parental consents have been obtained, gives you a great venue for thesis projects. The advantage of conducting such research is that you are the one who controls, to a great degree, the implementation of the study. From my experience, it is a great advantage not having to rely on another person for data collection. However, the type of problem studied will have to be something germane to the circumstances in your classroom. This may impact the study you conduct. For example, suppose you are interested in studying how a certain behavior management system alters the attention level of children with ADHD. Unfortunately, you do not have any such children in your own classroom. If you are set on conducting such a study, it will be necessary to find a research site that has these children. Only then can you investigate what instructional or management variables affect attention level in children with ADHD. As another example, if you are interested in discerning whether children with autism can exhibit more sophisticated language with incidental teaching methods than with play therapy techniques, you will need access to children with autism who are currently talking and you will need to be able to conduct such a study in their classroom(s).

The purpose of the thesis research study can vary. In some cases, the purpose of a given study is simply to demonstrate that some intervention or treatment is effective in solving some problem in classroom behavior or learning. In other cases, the purpose of a particular research study is to compare how certain levels of an independent variable affect the dependent variable. The research model that follows, originally introduced by Bailey and Bostow (1981, pp. 56–60), will be used to identify four purposes and types of applied research studies. Following a cursory presentation of the components of this model for building an evidence base, potential research studies are delineated with respect to the four areas of inquiry: demonstration research studies, parametric research studies, comparative research studies, and component analysis studies (where relevant).

## Demonstration Research Studies

Demonstration research is important as a first step in building a knowledge base. Demonstration research attempts to demonstrate the efficacy of various approaches on student learning and behavior. Demonstration studies are needed when little is known empirically about effective instructional methods or behavioral strategies in a given area of practice. Suppose someone designs an instructional program that is geared to developing algebra skills in students who have failed the course previously. The designer of this unique program believes that incorporating more real-life examples will be more effective in teaching these students than the usual "formulas" approach. A study would be conducted to demonstrate that the use of this particular instructional material increases algebra test scores in a select group of students, that is, those who have failed the course previously. It is important to select participants for this study that fit that criterion, that is, students who have failed algebra previously. Students who pass algebra the first time are apparently able to gain competence through the traditional approach and do not constitute the target students of interest (they are referred to as "wrong participants"; Bailey & Bostow, 1981, p. 107). Using them for this study would prove nothing of significance. In contrast, conducting a research study with students who have previously failed algebra addresses a significant presenting problem. An instructional program that is effective in developing competence in students who don't usually succeed with the traditional approaches is needed. If experimental research with this subgroup has been minimal to nonexistent, then demonstrating that some instructional procedure or package is effective is certainly a contribution to the knowledge base.

Once an initial study is completed and favorable results are obtained, replication of such a demonstration must occur if a substantial evidence base is to be produced. Replication studies involve a demonstration of the effect across many more students of this type as well as across a variety of different grade levels at which algebra is taken, for example, 9th grade, 10th grade, 8th grade. Demonstration studies and the subsequent replication studies provide evidence that an instructional procedure or treatment has an extensive and robust effect on target students.

Demonstration studies can also determine the conditions under which a procedure is ineffective. You often hear that studies that result in data illustrating that a procedure does not work are not valuable. But I beg to differ enthusiastically. Suppose a hypothetical social skills instructional program is found to be effective in changing the social behavior of children in the playground. This effect is found at many grade levels, and across students in a variety of school districts that span the states. Further, it is replicated by many different researchers across many different socioeconomic levels. However, finding out that this program does not work for a certain group of students may be just as valuable. Perhaps this program does not work for students who are asocial, that is, students who have few friends. When replication studies are conducted in schools where these asocial students exist, no effect is found with this subgroup. This finding points to the need for a different intervention in these circumstances and enhances the knowledge base. Demonstration studies demonstrate when a treatment is effective and when it is not (but some other procedure is shown to work).

## Comparative Research Studies

Areas where there exists a substantial number of demonstration research studies still require other, more complex empirical studies to expand the knowledge base. Other questions need to be answered. In the case of the unique algebra program, let's say that the researcher found that her instructional format and materials were effective in developing competence in algebra skills with the target students. Further, other researchers found this effect also, with different grade levels than the original study and different levels of student aptitude for algebra. In other words, there is significant evidence that this instructional format works for learners who do not achieve competence with the usual materials. The next set of research questions is as follows: Is this verified instructional method for teaching algebra more effective, and/or does it develop skills faster, than other approaches? In other words, at this point in the evolution of the knowledge base, the need is to determine whether the unique instructional procedure is more effective than alternative approaches or materials. For example, comparing this method of teaching algebra with the formulas method would be a good start. In this type of study, each participant in the study would be exposed to each treatment or experimental condition being tested. In that manner, an analysis of individual effects would reveal which procedure worked best for each student.

Comparative research is certainly needed with respect to the knowledge base in educational practice, since many proposed or suggested techniques often have little or no empirical backing. By conducting comparative research, ineffective methods can be exposed and hopefully discarded. Here is a poignant example of a comparative research study with respect to the effectiveness of two different instructional methods (Narayan, Heward, Gardner, Courson, & Omness, 1990). The need to engage students in instruction is well known as a requirement for student acquisition of skills. Unfortunately, many proposed or currently used techniques have never been subjected to empirical testing. They are taken as effective on a leap of faith by practitioners. One such technique used in classrooms across the country during lesson presentations is probably as old as the ancient Greeks such as Socrates. The teacher initiates the instructional presentation by presenting the lesson. To engage students, the teacher asks the class questions during the lesson presentation. Students raise their hands to respond to each question. Sounds good! As you can see, this format has been around for quite some time. But is it really more effective than other methods in getting student engagement and attention as well as in the acquisition of skills? In science, we address efficacy via experimental research data, not via a polling of people's opinions.

In a classic study, Narayan et al. (1990) compared two techniques via two experimental conditions: (1) hand raising (HR) and (2) response cards (RC). The students' scores on daily quiz grades in a social studies period in a fourth-grade class constituted the dependent variable for this study. The researchers compared these instructional conditions in an ABAB design. In the HR condition (Phase A), the teacher would ask a question and then call on someone who had a hand raised. The teacher would indicate whether the student's answer was right or wrong, and then proceed with more instruction or ask another question. In the RC condition (Phase B), all students responded to the teacher's question by writing their answer on their dry erase card and holding it up upon the command, "Ready, show!"

Which technique resulted in better quiz grades? The mean quiz grade for the first HR condition was 73%. The mean quiz grade for the first RC condition was 82%, almost a 10-point increase in test scores! This research finding has been demonstrated in other studies examining this comparison across other content areas (Armendariz & Umbreit, 1999; Cavanaugh, Heward, & Donelson, 1996; Christie & Schuster, 2003). While hand raising is as old as the hills, it does not match up to response cards as an instructional method to benefit student acquisition of academic skills. As is evident, comparative research can eventually lead to the validation of one methodology over others, in terms of efficacy.

## Parametric Research Studies

Testing the levels of a variable involved in a treatment program becomes a laudable research goal once demonstration studies have verified the efficacy of a technique. For example, let us say that a plethora of studies have established that exercise in the morning results in longer duration of sleep at night, for persons who have difficulty sleeping. However, one might pose the following question: How much exercise is needed to get at least 7 hours or more sleep a night? A parametric study might compare the effects of 20 minutes, versus half an hour, versus 1 hour of exercise in the morning as the dependent variable. Or it might compare the effects of vigorous and mild exercise on duration of sleep. As you can see, parametric studies address an important aspect of practice, that is, how much of a given intervention is needed.

This type of research question is very important in educational practice. You have probably heard that in order for time out to work, you must be consistent. But almost everyone is inconsistent to some degree. How inconsistent can a teacher or parent be in implementing time out and still yield a desirable effect? If parents catch one out of every three target behaviors, and send the child to time out, will time out work? What about implementing time out in one of every eight instances of target disruptive behavior?

A study by Clark, Rowbury, Baer, and Baer (1973) examined different levels of implementation of time out on the daily rates of disruptive behavior of a preschool child with special needs. The child was 8 years old but still attended a preschool program (remember, this study was conducted in the early 1970s). In the first experiment, the researchers demonstrated that a continuous schedule of time out was very effective in drastically reducing such target behavior when compared to the baseline condition. In the second experiment, a number of different schedules were compared. Experiment II provided some answers to the question, how consistent does one have to be? Several conditions involving a variable schedule of delivery of time out were compared. For example, a VR 4 translates to a time out being rendered on average every four incidents of disruptive behavior. A VR 8 would entail a time out being needed, on average, every eight incidents. The data for the mean rate of disruptive behavior for each condition are given in Table 5.1.

Table 5.1

### DATA ON INTERMITTENT SCHEDULES OF TIME-OUT DELIVERY

| SCHEDULE OF TIME-OUT DELIVERY/ DISRUPTIVE INCIDENT | MEAN RATE OF DISRUPTIVE BEHAVIOR/HOUR |
|---|---|
| VR 4 | 5.6 |
| VR 8 | 13.7 |
| VR 3 | 3.0 |
| DPH (Time out was delivered if rate exceeded certain number/hour) | 3.6 |

As is evident, a VR 8 produces a significant increase in disruptive behavior, making such inconsistency a problem in achieving effective treatment. In contrast, VR 3 and DPH schedules provide the best results, given a noncontinuous schedule (see Table 5.1). Apparently you can be a little inconsistent and still get decent results, but there is a limit to the degree of inconsistency.

Replication of parametric findings is just as important. Let's say that an initial study on the effects of an instructional program with ELL students found that using peer tutoring for 10 minutes was markedly more effective than using peer tutoring for a 3-minute period. This study was conducted with three ELL classes of third and fourth graders at a school district in suburban Dallas, Texas. Would you obtain similar results in Atlanta? How about inner-city schools in New York? Would this finding hold up at the junior high school level? What about high school? This is where theses and dissertations come in. They provide a valuable contribution to the literature base by extending these findings in the aforementioned areas.

## Component Analysis

Many intervention programs involve multiple components. A component analysis attempts to discern which components are primarily responsible for producing the change in learning and/or behavior. These types of research studies are usually conducted after an initial knowledge base is developed with respect to an intervention package.

Here is a prime example of a component analysis. A study compared the differential effectiveness of two components added to a package treatment on reading decoding skills in context (Nelson, Alber, & Gordy, 2007). Four students with mild disabilities served as participants for this component analysis study. The dependent variables were: (1) number of words read correctly in context per minute, and (2) number of errors per minute. Following a baseline condition, systematic error correction (EC) procedures were instituted in a multiple baseline across participants design. Following this condition, repeated readings (RR) were added to the EC procedure. Subsequent to those two components being implemented in a multiple baseline design, reading prior passages was added to the EC and RR components. The results demonstrated the greater effectiveness of the three components in the package in contrast to any of the prior conditions on both dependent variables, with progressively more difficult reading material. Table 5.2 illustrates the increase in number of words read correctly for one student (Alex).

Table 5.2

**EFFECTS OF DIFFERENT COMPONENTS ON THE DEPENDENT VARIABLE**

| EXPERIMENTAL CONDITION | NO. WORDS CORRECT/MIN (RANGE) |
| --- | --- |
| Baseline | 15–45 |
| EC | 30–50 |
| EC and RR | 60–70 |
| Package | 60–70 (except for one low data point) |

## The Need for Replication Studies:
## The Value of Your Thesis Project

Building a knowledge base in a given field is a lengthy and arduous process, and one that is not based on just one major study. While the homogeneity of groups can be minimal with respect to the phenomena studied by natural scientists, such is not the case with humans. Therefore, it is imperative that a knowledge base is developed by systematic replication of findings. While many students have heard that to duplicate a study done by someone else is not worthy of being called research, this could not be further from the truth!

Many students are led to believe that their study must find a new cure for some existing problem. But graduate theses that address instructional and behavioral interventions that have already been verified are needed. Such studies might investigate the effectiveness of the procedure in a slightly different context, or with a slightly different target population, and/or collect multiple dependent variables. As you can see, all these potential investigations are needed for science to progress. The development of a sound methodology for addressing classroom and educational problems requires numerous replications of effects. For example, the existent research on the effects of token reinforcement contingencies on child and adult behavior is extensive. There are decades of research, dating back to the 1960s, attesting to the efficacy of such a treatment on behavior. To dismiss someone's claim that token reinforcement is not supported by extensive research might have been plausible in 1963, but not in the year 2009! Numerous researchers have found that designing a token economy strengthens the target behaviors incorporated in it. The effects of token economies have been validated across students from many grade levels, in both general and special education classes, in their homes, in facilities and other residential settings, and so forth. This replication across many different research studies demonstrated that the effects occurred regardless of the particular student involved, who the teacher was, who the researcher was, where the study took place, and who the particular data collectors were. To build a knowledge base, one must have replication of research results. Enter your thesis project.

## POTENTIAL THESIS/DISSERTATION RESEARCH TOPICS

In the remainder of this chapter, I present a number of potential research studies with respect to a variety of classroom management and instructional interventions. A uniform format is provided for each intervention. Prior to a delineation of potential research studies, the intervention is presented in brief format so that the user can develop a basic knowledge base for the various classroom management and instructional interventions.

Each research topic then examines possible research proposals involving demonstration of effect studies, comparative research, parametric studies, and finally component analyses.

---

## DAILY REPORT CARD (DRC)

### Suggested Readings

Atkeson, B. M., & Forehand, R. (1979). Home-based reinforcement designed to modify classroom behaviors. *Psychological Bulletin, 86,* 1298–1309.

Bailey, J. S., Wolf, M. M., & Phillips, E. C. (1970). Home-based reinforcement and the modification of pre-delinquents' classroom behavior. *Journal of Applied Behavior Analysis, 3,* 183–184.

Cipani, E. (1999). Parent solution for school related problems: The daily report card. In E. Cipani (Ed.), *Helping parents help their kids: A clinical guide for six problem behaviors* (pp. 87–107). Philadelphia, PA: Routledge.

Schumaker, J. B., Hovell, M. F., & Shreman, J. A. (1977). An analysis of daily report cards and parent-managed privileges in the improvement of adolescents' classroom performance. *Journal of Applied Behavior Analysis, 10,* 449–464.

Trice, A. D., Parker, F. C., Furrow, F., & Iwata, B. A. (1983). An analysis of home contingencies to improve school behavior with disruptive adolescents. *Education and Treatment of Children, 6,* 389–399.

## Brief Description

The daily report card (DRC) provides a system of monitoring student behavior at school with contingent reinforcement. It is more commonly known in the research literature as a home-based reinforcement system (Cipani, 1999). The student's target behavior at school is monitored by the teacher, and the results are transmitted to the parents daily. The delivery of reinforcement contingencies for each day's performance occurs at home. Hence, reinforcement is delivered in the home for behavior that occurred at school.

What is the advantage of such a system? With a home-based reinforcement system, more powerful or unique reinforcers, only available at home, may be used to influence a student's behavior at school. For example, TV time, talking to friends on the phone, and computer time for noneducational activities can all be used as contingencies for school performance. This makes students accountable to their parents for their behavior at school.

The program works like this. Daily results are transmitted to the home via a DRC. This DRC indicates the level of the selected target behavior(s) during the school day. The data collection system designed for the DRC should be ecologically friendly, that is, a teacher should be able to measure the behavior without significant interference with his or her teaching and other classroom duties. Upon receipt of the DRC, the parent compares this information with a preset standard for reinforcement. For example, the standard for earning computer time might be six or fewer occurrences of a target behavior. If the student achieves the level necessary for reinforcement, that is, has four occurrences on a given day, the designated reinforcers are delivered in the home by the parent. This program can target desirable school behavior(s) for increase, as well as undesirable behaviors for decrease.

The DRC is useful with students who are capable of delaying access to powerful reinforcement until later in the day (e.g., when they get home). It is not indicated for students who need more immediate access to tangible reinforcers or shorter work periods. Parental and teacher cooperation is essential. However, if it is appropriate, the DRC may influence behavior in a more dramatic manner by providing powerful reinforcers for meeting behavioral criteria for reinforcement set at school. It also is an excellent method for getting parents involved in their child's school behavior.

The DRC does have a significant drawback: parent implementation (or lack thereof) of designated contingencies. In order for the DRC to be effective, parents must provide the designated reinforcer when the child earns it through his or her behavior at school and withhold it when the child's behavior does not meet the criteria. If the delivery of such contingencies is not produced, then the DRC is only a feedback system at best. It may be difficult for you to ascertain if a parent is implementing the home-based reinforcement plan, which can certainly affect the data you obtain. You may not get an effect on student behavior, not because the DRC is ineffective, but rather because of poor (or nonexistent) implementation.

## Procedures for Implementation

1. Identify target behavior(s), which can be both desirable classroom behaviors and inappropriate problem behaviors. In the beginning, try focusing on just one or possibly two target behaviors.
2. If the DRC is targeting and therefore monitoring appropriate behavior, it may be more feasible to use some form of interval system. Identify the number of intervals the school day will be divided into. Within each interval, the teacher merely determines whether the target behavior occurred or did not occur (i.e., it is not necessary to count each occurrence). If the target behavior is an undesirable behavior that is conspicuous in its occurrence, it can possibly be measured via frequency counts.
3. Design a home-based DRC that lists the target behavior(s) and indicates the status of the appropriate behavior for each interval. If measuring frequency, select no more than two behaviors to list on the report card.
4. Collect baseline data using the DRC form.
5. Assign points for the occurrence of a target appropriate behavior within each interval (e.g., 3 points if the student finishes all work assigned during that interval). You can also assign a loss of points for target problem behaviors that occur within each interval (e.g., 5 points if the student disrupts class during the interval).
6. Determine the point value needed for the student's access to the backup tangible reinforcer for each day (e.g., 15 total points).
7. Meet with the teacher, the parent, and the student to go over the target behavior(s) in the system and the backup reinforcer(s) to be used.

## Hypothetical Example of Implementation: Disruptive Behavior

Johnny's third-grade teacher implements a home-based reinforcement system with regard to his disruptive behavior at school by designing a card with the following values: (a) zero, (b) one to two, and (c) three or more. At the end of the day, the teacher marks the category that details the number of disruptive behavior incidents Johnny had that day. When Johnny brings home the card, his mother examines the information. If it is marked with zero occurrences for that day, he earns an extra half-hour of time to stay up after his scheduled 8:00 p.m. bedtime. If it is marked with one to two occurrences, he goes to bed 15 minutes early. If it is marked with three or more, he goes to bed an hour early.

## Hypothetical Example of Implementation: Turning in Homework Assignments

Sarah's fifth-grade teacher notes that her grade has suffered because she does not turn in her homework assignments regularly. She meets with Sarah's mom, and they identify a DRC system to address the fact that Sarah loves to text chat with her friends on the phone, and her mom agrees that such an activity should be a privilege, not a right. The DRC has the following scoring method: (a) turned in all homework; (b) turned in all but one of her assignments; (c) failed to turn in most of her assignments (more than one) or turned in none at all; or (d) did not have any homework due. At the end of the day, the teacher marks the category that fits Sarah's performance. When Sarah brings home the card, her mother examines the information. If she turned in all her homework, or did not have any assignments that day, her texting of friends is limited only by the phone plan she is on. If she missed only one assignment, she can have only 5 minutes texting that day, and she must show all her completed assignments to her mother that night before getting her 5 minutes. If she failed to turn in most of her assignments, she loses all her phone privileges, as well as her computer time, and must finish her assignments before 7:00 p.m. that evening. To aid in the behavior of turning in all assignments, each night Sarah and her mother put all the homework assignments due the next school day in a special folder.

## Demonstration Research Studies

After conducting a review of the existing literature, you may see a need to conduct a study to test the efficacy of the DRC across different target problem behaviors from those already examined. The literature on the use of the DRC to increase appropriate behavior may be sparse and provide an area for a thesis or dissertation. For example, one topic of study may be to evaluate the effectiveness of the DRC in increasing a student's cooperation during cleanup times after art activities (when compared with a control condition). Additional studies demonstrating the efficacy of the DRC on appropriate behaviors such as completing assignments and following directions, as well as problem behaviors, for example, out-of-seat behaviors, leaving the room without authorization, refusing to do class assignments, and so forth, may prove to be a valuable empirical contribution. If you select different behaviors with the same student, a multiple baseline across behaviors design would be perfect. You could also use a reversal design and alternate the DRC with the lack of the DRC for the same target behavior. You would implement the DRC after a baseline on the target behavior(s) for several weeks. Once you have a stable set of data for this first experimental condition, you would reverse the condition, removing the DRC (make sure you arrange this aspect with the parents beforehand). Especially if the DRC was effective, this condition might be kept short if the target behavior reappears quickly at baseline levels. Upon stability being achieved, you could then return to the DRC.

The demonstration of the efficacy of the DRC can also be tested with different grade levels from those that the current research has examined, as well as with students with varying mental and developmental disorders, for example, students with ADHD, learning disabilities, and mild mental retardation, remedial readers, and gifted students (who may not turn in their homework), and so on.

## Comparative Research Studies

The research testing various other behavior management procedures for implementation against the DRC might be drawn from what the target students have already been exposed to. For example, if the parent agrees, a student whose behavior has led to suspensions might be a good candidate for a DRC. The results obtained under DRC conditions can be compared with the prior use of suspensions only. Other test conditions to compare the DRC against can be drawn from what is currently being implemented, for example, weekly counseling, meetings with the principal, and other usual procedures for implementation.

In a comparative research study, it may be difficult to get the school personnel to agree to terminate the current procedures for implementation for the sake of the research findings. This can be overcome by using an ABAB reversal design and implementing the DRC in Condition B, on top of the already used strategy or strategies. It would be important to document, via data, the level of the existing strategies across all control and experimental conditions, to ensure that this variable did not vary significantly.

Table 5.3 provides a pictorial representation of this potential ABAB study. The first row depicts the experimental condition (i.e., ABAB). The second row delineates the experimental procedures for implementation, either baseline, which involves implementing the current strategies (A), or a package that includes the current strategies plus the DRC (B). The last row depicts the resulting data, demonstrating a change in behavior as a function of change in conditions.

Again, it may be difficult to get a true comparison of the DRC with another strategy, especially if the strategy is currently being deployed. Hence, your study must deploy that strategy (or those strategies) across the length of the research. However, with the use of a reversal design,

Table 5.3

## AN ABAB DESIGN

| Experimental condition | Condition A: Current strategies (visits with principal, counseling sessions) | Condition B: In addition to strategies used in A, DRC added | Condition A: Replicate prior A | Condition B: Replicate prior B |
|---|---|---|---|---|
| Data collection | Collect data on target behaviors under current conditions | Collect data on target behaviors under existing strategies and addition of DRC | Collect data on target behaviors under prior usual conditions | Collect data on target behaviors under existing strategies and addition of DRC |
| Possible effect on data | Baseline data | Behavior changes in desirable direction | Rate of behavior returns to baseline levels | Behavior changes again in desired direction, which demonstrates that desired results obtained when DRC in effect[a] |

[a]You may then want to convince school personnel to drop their prior strategy; show data regarding the ineffectiveness of this strategy.

you can add the DRC during the B conditions to produce a cause-and-effect design. You may then demonstrate that the prior strategies result in rates of behavior that are not significant, when compared with a norm standard, and therefore not desirable (i.e., data under A conditions). Only when the DRC is added does behavior change in the desired direction.

## REINFORCEMENT PROGRAMS WITH A RESPONSE COST (RC)

### Suggested Readings

Iwata, B. A., & Bailey, J. S. (1974). Reward vs. cost token systems: An analysis of the effects on students and teacher. *Journal of Applied Behavior Analysis, 7,* 567–576.

Musser, E. H., Bray, M. A., Kehle, T. J., & Jenson, W. R. (2001). Reducing disruptive behaviors in students with serious emotional disturbance. *School Psychology Review, 30,* 294–304.

Pfiffner, L. J., & O'Leary, S. G. (1987). The efficacy of all-positive management as a function of the prior use of negative consequences. *Journal of Applied Behavioral Analysis, 20,* 265–271.

Rapport, M. D., Murphy, H. A., & Bailey, J. S. (1982). Ritalin vs. response cost in the control of hyperactive children: A within-subject comparison. *Journal of Applied Behavior Analysis, 15,* 205–216.

### Brief Description

Very often, point deductions (fines) are a major method of attempting to change a student's undesirable behavior. This method is more technically termed *response cost* (RC), with a sizable literature demonstrating the efficacy of such a contingency in the behavioral journals. RC provides a method for providing reinforcement for appropriate behaviors as well as a response cost contingency for targeting undesirable behaviors within a token system. Of course, fines are only useful if the students are given a mechanism for earning points for desirable behavior. The reinforcement program should allow students to accrue points rapidly for appropriate behavior. Therefore, the teacher has to implement a program where there exists a substantial payoff for appropriate behaviors (tokens, points, checks toward completion).

If a point system for appropriate behavior is not in place, the teacher can still use an RC system. In this version, the student would begin each day with an allotted stipend of points. Subsequently, undesirable target behaviors would produce a fine, deducted from the initial stipend.

The points remaining at the end of the day are then traded in for designated reinforcers.

Do not use an RC component where the student is not capable of earning a sufficient number of points or tokens for exhibiting appropriate behaviors. Students who go into significant negative point values quickly lose their motivation to earn points (e.g., when a student is –350 points, he or she is too far behind to catch up and earn reinforcement). In that regard, set a limit on the number of times a fine can be levied for a specific behavioral incident, so that the student cannot lose all the points he or she has earned over a several-day period because of a 5-minute blow-up. Utilize some time out or removal from the current environment under those circumstances.

## Procedures for Implementation

1. Identify one target behavior or several target behaviors that result in a fine (RC procedure) and target the student(s) or the entire class.
2. Implement the reinforcement program for appropriate behavior (i.e., number of points given for each occurrence), or designate the initial stipend beginning each day or period.
3. Designate the reinforcers to be earned as well as the cost of these backup reinforcers.
4. Using baseline data, identify how many points will be taken away (i.e., fined) for the occurrence of a single target behavior or target behaviors.
5. Identify how many fines will occur in a short time period before moving to a backup contingency (e.g., time out or removal).
6. Apply RC each time behavior occurs, unless a backup contingency is necessary when reaching the limit of fines allowed (see brief discussion above).
7. Evaluate the effectiveness of the program on the basis of the change in rate of target behavior(s) from the baseline.

## Hypothetical Example of Implementation: In-Seat and Attending Behavior

Roger's special day class teacher develops a token system for appropriate in-seat and attending behaviors. Given Roger's current limited attention span, the amount of attending behavior that is required for reinforcement is initially kept short (e.g., 5 minutes using a timer). Whenever Roger is in his seat and attends for the entire length of the time, he earns 5 points. If he engages in out-of-seat behavior or disengages from the task assignment, the timer is reset for 5 minutes. This contingency seems well suited to handling out-of-seat behavior as well as attention to task. However, Roger also engages in taunting comments toward junior high school peers. Roger's teacher also wishes to decrease his taunting comments but allows the reinforcement plan to begin to influence his seat work first. Following three weeks of implementation of the reinforcement plan for out-of-seat and attending behaviors, Roger's teacher designates an RC for taunting comments. For each incident involving taunting a peer, Roger loses three points. The teacher imposes a maximum of four fines in a 1-hour period. Once four fines have been levied, Roger will be in a time out from earning or losing points, until the next hour (when the slate is wiped clean).

## Hypothetical Example of Implementation: Verbally Aggressive Incidents in the Playground

A sixth-grade teacher has received reports from the playground supervisor that multiple students in her class are saying inappropriate things to each other during the playground recess. The teacher inquires what the current practice is for handling such a behavior. She learns that in some cases, the playground supervisor will call the student over to her and give him or her a warning. In other cases, particularly if the student has been warned previously in that same recess period, he or she is placed "on the wall." This basically constitutes a brief time out from play activities. In summary, sometimes a warning occurs and sometimes a time out (of unknown length) is the contingency. Therefore, the brief time out is not consistent. It would be more effective to attempt to get the adult supervisors to be more consistent in implementing time outs, that is, time out for each incident. However, discussions about this need for consistency have not proved fruitful in the past. The teacher decides to implement an RC contingency in the classroom that will add on to the current strategy.

Each day, each student in her class begins with 10 points on his or her recess card. If students are placed on the wall at any time during their recess, they lose all 10 points. If students are given a warning, they lose 5 points; with more than one warning, they lose all 10 points. In order to have 10 minutes of preferred activity at the end of the day, students must keep all 10 points. If students have only 5 points, they may have only 3 minutes of preferred activity at the end of the day. They will have to work until the last 3 minutes of class before getting their preferred-activity time.

## Demonstration Research Studies

Following a review of the existing literature, a thesis or dissertation study may test the efficacy of RC with different grade levels from those that the current research has examined. Another area of demonstration research would be testing RC with students with mental disorders that have not received significant research attention. While there may be an existent knowledge base for how RC works for children with ADHD, learning disabilities, and mild mental retardation, can the same be said for remedial readers, gifted students (who may not turn in their homework), and others? Another area for demonstration research studies may be the application of RC in different contexts within the school setting, for example, recess, physical education class, assemblies, school outings, and so forth.

## Comparative Research Studies

Research testing various behavior management strategies may prove a valuable area of inquiry. Too often, strategies that are used have had little or no empirical testing. Comparing those techniques with RC would constitute a valuable contribution to the research literature. Procedures to test against RC might be drawn from what the target students have already been exposed to. For example, students whose behavior has led to suspensions might be good candidates for a study comparing suspensions and RC. The results obtained under RC conditions can be compared with the prior use of suspensions only (a multiple baseline across participants design might be well suited). Other test conditions to which to compare RC might be weekly counseling, meetings with the principal, or other usual procedures. Counseling with disruptive students is widespread but not often tested against a strategy such as RC and reinforcement.

In a comparative study, it may be difficult to get the school personnel to agree to terminate the current procedures for implementation for the sake of the research findings. This can be overcome by using an ABAB reversal design, and implementing the RC in the B condition, on top of the already used strategy (or strategies). It would be important to document, via data, the level of the existing strategies across all control and experimental conditions, to ensure that this variable did not vary.

Table 5.4 provides a pictorial representation of this potential study. The first row depicts the experimental condition (i.e., ABAB). The second row delineates the experimental procedures for implementation, either baseline, which involves implementing the current strategies (A), or a package that includes the current strategies plus RC (B). The last row depicts the resulting data, demonstrating a change in behavior as a function of a change in conditions.

Again, it may be difficult to get a true comparison of RC against another strategy, especially if the strategy is currently being deployed. Hence, your study must deploy that strategy (or strategies) across the length of the research. However, with the use of a reversal design, you can add the RC during the B conditions to produce a cause-and-effect design. You may then demonstrate that the prior strategies resulted in rates of behavior that were not significantly improved when compared

## Table 5.4

### POTENTIAL STUDY OF RESPONSE COST (RC)

| Experimental Condition | Condition A: Current strategies (visits with principal, counseling sessions) | Condition B: In addition to strategies used in A, RC added | Condition A: Replicate prior A | Condition B: Replicate prior B |
|---|---|---|---|---|
| Data collection | Collect data on target behaviors under current conditions | Collect data on target behaviors under existing strategies and addition of RC | | Collect data on target behaviors under existing strategies and addition of RC |
| Possible effect on data | Baseline data | Behavior changes in desirable direction | Rate of behavior returns to baseline levels | Behavior changes again in desired direction, desired results obtained when DRC is in effect[a] |

[a]You may then want to convince school personnel to drop their prior strategy; show data regarding the ineffectiveness of this strategy.

Table 5.5

| MULTIELEMENT DESIGN TESTING THREE TREATMENTS | | | |
|---|---|---|---|
| **PHASE 1** | **PHASE 2** | **PHASE 3** | **PHASE 4** |
| Baseline | Alternate the three conditions in quick-switching fashion | Reversal (short) | Implementation of most effective treatment from Phase 2 |

against a norm standard for such behavior and hence were not desirable (i.e., data under A conditions). Only when RC is added does behavior change to a level where the target behavior is occurring at a level that is appropriate.

Another area for comparison is RC against procedures that have been deemed as constituting an all-positive approach (see Pffifner & O'Leary, 1987). For example, in a multielement design, RC could be one condition, baseline could be another, and the use of positive statements and rule reminders could be a third condition (see Table 5.5).

## Parametric Studies

There is a great need to evaluate behavioral contingencies in terms of the effectiveness of consequences under less than consistent delivery. The applied field often has difficulty with the implementation of a contingent procedure, in comparison to research facilities. In university research studies, the ability to consistently implement a procedure and collect reliable data is aided by additional personnel resources, which are not available in everyday classrooms. The question of whether an experimental effect can occur with a procedure that has been verified as efficacious but is implemented at a lowered percentage of implementation is an area for parametric research.

For example, a parametric study might involve a comparison of the dependent variable of RC at 100% implementation (i.e., a fine for each occurrence) with RC at 50% implementation (i.e., a fine for every other occurrence). Of course, different parametric analyses than these can be selected, which answer the basic question, "How inconsistent can you be and still get a behavioral effect?" A sample comparison of a parametric study with three values (100%, 50%, and 33%) in an ABCADCA design is delineated in Table 5.6.

Table 5.6

| PARAMETRIC STUDY OF RESPONSE COST (RC) | | | | | | |
|---|---|---|---|---|---|---|
| **BASELINE (A)** | **RC 1 (B)** | **RC 2 (C)** | **RC 1 (B)** | **RC 3 (D)** | **RC 2 (C)** | **RC 1 (B)** |
| Use of token system only | RC at 100% implementation | RC at 50% | | RC at 33% | | |

## TAP ME ON THE SHOULDER!: TEACHING APPROPRIATE ATTENTION-GETTING BEHAVIOR

### Suggested Readings

Cipani, E. (1988). The missing item format. *Teaching Exceptional Children, 21,* 25–27.

Cipani, E. (1990). Excuse me, I'll have . . . Teaching appropriate attention getting behavior to young children with severe handicaps. *Mental Retardation, 28,* 29–83.

Laski, K. E., Charlop, M. H., & Schreibman, L. (1988). Training parents to use the natural language paradigm to increase their autistic children's speech. *Journal of Applied Behavior Analysis, 21,* 391–400.

Tirapelle, L., & Cipani, E. (1992). Developing functional requesting: Acquisition, durability and generalization of effects. *Exceptional Children, 58,* 260–269.

### Brief Description

Many students with severe disabilities are not capable of getting someone's attention (appropriately) when they need to communicate, unless they are face to face with the teacher or adult. The students wish to indicate their needs or desires to the teacher, but they are unable to engage in appropriate attention-getting behavior to make their request. Instead, they will either simply sit there until someone comes over, or they will engage in an inappropriate behavior, such as tantrum or self-abuse. This inability to get someone's attention can often lead to the conditions under which behavior problems develop and flourish in classrooms serving these students. What is needed is a teaching procedure that develops an attention-getting response. This behavior allows the student who is capable of making requests to get the teacher's attention when he or she is involved in an activity with someone else or something else.

This procedure is a systematic method for teaching students to gain the teacher's attention when the teacher is not in close proximity.

It teaches a chain of behaviors starting with the teacher, approaching the teacher and then tapping the teacher on the shoulder to get her or his initial attention. Once the teacher attends to the student as a result of this behavior, the student then makes a request or statement. This procedure utilizes prompting and stimulus-fading techniques to develop the chain of appropriate attention-getting behaviors.

## Procedures for Implementation

1. Develop several requesting and/or protesting skills.
2. Ensure that the student wants or needs something by withholding it, in order to develop requesting skills. If you are attempting to develop appropriate attention-getting skills for protesting undesired events or activities, than you need to present such an undesired event and then immediately leave the area (see Cipani, 1988, the missing-item format).
3. Face away from the student and gesture to him or her to tap you on the arm.
4. Contingent upon the student tapping your arm (each time), turn and face the student and ask "What do you want?"
5. Reinforce the student's request by providing the desired item or removing the undesired item or event.
6. Repeat the above procedures for implementation several times (discrete trial format) until arm tapping is occurring consistently.
7. Move 1–2 feet away, then gesture for the student to tap your arm.
8. Reinforce the student's chain of behaviors involving walking toward you and tapping you on the arm by saying, "What do you want?" Repeat steps 5–6.
9. Alter your distance from the student in each consecutive session, so that eventually the student can walk up to you, wherever you are in the classroom area, or other room, and exhibit appropriate attention-getting behavior.

## Hypothetical Example of Implementation: Attention-Getting Skills

Mary's special day class teacher, Ms. Thomas, wants to teach Mary how to get her attention when Mary wants something and is not in the teacher's immediate area. She sets up a situation where she asks Mary to comply with some request, for example, "Go hang up your coat on the rack." Ms. Thomas makes sure that Mary needs some item in order to comply with her request; for example, she removes a hanger. Ms. Thomas then gestures Mary to tap her on the shoulder (or say "teacher"). When Mary performs this behavior, the teacher turns to her and asks her what she wants. When Mary requests the hanger (vocal as well as nonvocal communication methods could be used), the teacher gives the hanger to Mary. Ms. Thomas utilizes this missing-item format (see Cipani, 1988) for many other items. She gradually increases the distance she moves away from Mary so that Mary must learn how to locate the teacher in the room, tap her on the shoulder, and then when recognized make her request. Eventually, this generalizes to times when Mary wants other items or activities in the absence of a teacher request for compliance.

## Demonstration Research Studies

After reviewing the existing literature, you may find that more research demonstrating the efficacy of these teaching procedures could be done with regard to developing protesting behavior. It is essential for the field to have replication studies, that is, to replicate procedures found effective in some studies with different participants, behaviors, and so on, to build a solid evidence base for teaching practice. For example, the procedures for teaching the protesting of nonpreferred items may have been conducted with several students with autism. However, systematic replication with other types of students with severe disabilities, for example, students with mental retardation, students with Down syndrome, brain-injured students, and students with selective mutism, may not have been conducted. Therefore, conducting a study that verifies that such procedures lead to protesting combined with the concurrent development of attention-getting behavior would be important. The attention-getting component can also be used for specific protesting or requesting behaviors that have been examined in the professional literature, for example, in a study that developed protesting an unfair criticism, requesting (negotiating) a certain amount of a work task, and so forth.

Further, additional studies with students with autism may be conducted where the students in your study vary slightly from the characteristics delineated in prior research. If prior studies demonstrated that the procedure works with students in a special day class setting, your study could test the procedure for implementation with students who are educated in a mainstream environment. Additionally, a difference in who is carrying out the procedure could fill a void in the literature. Researching the use of personnel other than special education teachers would be a great contribution to the literature.

## Component Analysis Studies

The procedure for developing attention-getting behavior has multiple steps or components. The efficacy of using the entire package could be tested against the use of just one or several steps. For example, you could compare the discrete trial package delineated above with an incidental teaching approach on the development of the attention-getting behavior. Which one produces a faster result? Which one produces a larger percentage of correct behaviors? Which one produces a larger number of inappropriate problem behaviors?

## Parametric Studies

In this type of research, one would test how often an adult's attention and mediation of the attention-getting response are required to obtain an initial effect and subsequent maintenance of the behavior. In obtaining the acquisition of attention-getting behavior, does the rate of mediation of the behavior have to be at 100% for acquisition to occur? In many settings, this may prove to be unfeasible to implement. A study that determines the values at which such a teaching procedure is rendered ineffective would be a valuable contribution.

For example, you could conduct the following study: In one condition, provide teacher attention and mediation of the student's attention-getting behavior at 100% levels (i.e., every single time the behavior occurs). In the other experimental condition, the student's behavior would be mediated at only 50% levels. What is the differential effect on acquisition of the attention-getting behavior between both conditions, if any? This answers a very pragmatic question that is relevant for everyday practice: How inconsistent can staff be and still develop the desired behavior? Of course, other studies would then be needed to determine if, say, a 30% level is effective during the acquisition phase of training. It would be important not to use a reversal or alternating treatments design in this research, because of the irreversibility of the behavior once acquired. Some form of multiple baseline design across different participants would be most suitable. A multiple baseline design across settings or behaviors may also create a problem: carryover to untreated baselines.

## SELF-MONITORING OF APPROPRIATE OR INAPPROPRIATE BEHAVIOR

### Suggested Readings

Cooper, J. O., Heron, T. E., & Heward, W. L. (2007). Self-management. In J. O. Cooper, T. E. Heron, & W. L. Heward (Eds.), *Applied behavior analysis* (2nd ed., pp. 575–612). Upper Saddle River, NJ: Pearson Education.

Felixbrod, J. J., & O'Leary, K. D. (1973). Effects of reinforcement on children's academic behavior as a function of self-determined and externally determined and externally imposed contingencies. *Journal of Applied Behavior Analysis, 6,* 241–250.

Hughes, C. A., & Hendrickson, J. M. (1987). Self-monitoring with at-risk students in the regular class. *Education and Treatment of Children, 10,* 225–236.

Keller, C. L., Brady, M. P., & Taylor, R. L. (2005). Using self-evaluation to improve student teacher interns' use of specific praise. *Education and Training in Mental Retardation and Developmental Disabilities, 40,* 368–376.

Koegel, R. L., & Koegel, L. K. (1990). Extended reductions in stereotypic behavior of students with autism through a self-management treatment package. *Journal of Applied Behavior Analysis, 21,* 119–127.

Lloyd, J. W., Batemna, D. F., Landrum, T. J., & Hallahan, D. P. (1989). Self-recording of attention versus productivity. *Journal of Applied Behavior Analysis, 22,* 315–323.

McLaughlin, T. F., Burgess, N., & Sackville-West, L. (1981). Effects of self-recording plus matching on academic performance. *Child Behavior Therapy, 3,* 17–27.

Ninness, H. A. C., Fuerst, J., & Rutherford, R. D. (1991). Effects of self-management training and reinforcement on the transfer of improved conduct in the absence of supervision. *Journal of Applied Behavior Analysis, 24,* 479–508.

### Brief Description

Teaching students to self-manage their behavior is a critical step in their development as lifelong learners and responsible adults. Developing self-management begins with teaching students to self-monitor occurrences of behavior, then to self-determine consequences for their behavior, and finally to self-administer consequences. This program provides a basis for teaching the student or students to self-monitor their performance, be it in appropriate or problem behaviors. The teacher designates a system for monitoring the target behavior, either as a frequency count or as a momentary time sampling, as in the beeper system (see Cipani, 2008). The student identifies whether the target behavior occurred and records it on the self-monitoring sheet. The accuracy of such self-recordings can be checked. Once self-monitoring of behavior is accurate, other aspects of self-management can be introduced. The student may determine the standard for reinforcement (self-determine consequences) and also determine whether the standard has been met and deliver the reinforcer (self-deliver consequences). This program can be used in classroom and community settings.

## Procedures for Implementation

1. Identify the appropriate behavior(s) targeted for increase (or decrease in the case of inappropriate behaviors).
2. Teach the student to identify the occurrence of the target behavior(s) by listing specific examples or incidents of such behavior(s).
3. Teach the student how to record the target behaviors (e.g., frequency count or occurrence of behavior at the time of monitoring) on the self-recording data sheet.
4. Teach the student how to sum the frequency data and compare it with the selected standard.
5. Review the data with the student, with suggestions for improving performance.
6. Verbally reinforce accurate recording of target behavior(s). Random spot checks by the teacher or the therapist to ensure accurate self-recording can be utilized. Significant discrepancies between student and teacher evaluations can be cause for program revision, possibly reverting to teacher-administered evaluations for a time period or specifying contingencies for such discrepancies.

## Hypothetical Example of Implementation: Loud Talking

Johnny's teacher implements a self-monitoring system for his loud talking behavior at school by designing a card that has numbers 1–6 marked on it. Each time Johnny engages in loud talking, he marks a consecutive number on the card. The teacher reviews the data sheet with Johnny and also explains what are instances of loud talking. After each period, the teacher reviews the self-recordings and compares Johnny's recordings with the teacher's recordings of instances of loud talking. After a week of comparison and baseline, the reinforcement portion is implemented.

If Johnny marks two or fewer instances per class period (and is accurate), he earns 10 minutes of conversation time with a friend at the end of the day. If he goes over two instances in just one period he gets only half of the conversation time. If he goes over two instances more than once a day he does not get any conversation time that day and must work on an extra assignment during the conversation period instead. The teacher spot checks to ensure accuracy of self-recording and self-administration of reinforcement. Failure to mark accurately (there should be no more than one mistake in any one period) results in the teacher placing two additional marks in the period where the mistake occurred. Having a discrepancy in more than two periods will possibly result in loss of conversation time.

## Hypothetical Example of Implementation: Two Low-Performing Students

Mr. Roberts is considering using the beeper system (see Cipani, 2008) for two students in his eighth-grade class who have unacceptable levels of on-task behavior. On some days, it seems these two students are not engaged at all! He designs a data collection sheet with 20 data entry spots. He divides the 1-hour period into two 20-minute periods (with a 10-minute break in between). He wants to have 10 signals occur during each 20-minute period, meaning that the vibrating signal will be sent to him about every 2 minutes on average. He spends time in the first week of the program teaching both students what on-task behavior is and how they are to judge this when he says, "OK, record your behavior, line ___." They will score whether they were on task or not at that moment on the line delineated by Mr. Roberts. If the student was on task he will record a 1 for that line. If he was not on task at that time he will record a 0 on that line. Once the students understand the recording of on-task behavior, Mr. Roberts has them self-monitor for the first week. Of course he will compare their results with his own at the end of each period and keep monitoring each self-recording during this teaching phase. Once the students are recording accurately, he begins Phase 2, which is to provide reinforcement for acceptable levels of on-task behavior.

To determine the initial behavior standard, Mr. Roberts reviews his baseline data on the two students. The baseline data indicate that Student 1 ranges from a low of 5 points to a high of 11 points, with a mean of 8. Student 2 has a low of 5 and a high of 7, with a mean of 6. Mr. Roberts sets one standard for Student 1, which is 8 points or better, and a second standard for Student 2, which is 7 or better. If the behavior standard is met, the student gets 5 minutes of a preferred activity at the end of the first period on the next day. If the students earn 4 points more than the standard, they get an alternate activity after each period the following day. If they do not earn an alternate activity in either period the following day, they will continue working.

Mr. Roberts puts his plan in place and evaluates the students' accuracy of self-recording and their progress. After 2 weeks of implementation, he is pleased with the results. Both students have done so well that the behavior standard is now 13 for Student 1 and 9 for Student 2. Further, there was only one period where Student 1 had results that were discrepant from Mr. Roberts's results.

## Demonstration Research Studies

After a review of the existing literature is undertaken, additional research studies assessing the efficacy of self-monitoring may be needed at different grade levels, for different types of problem behaviors, or with regard to different applications for appropriate behaviors. For example, have there been sufficient studies conducted to assess self-monitoring in young children, children in middle school, or children in high school? What are the effects of self-monitoring on achievement test grades?

Probably a major area for demonstration research is to determine how student self-recordings can be made accurate, and how such accuracy can be maintained over time. How often do spot checks have to be performed in order to establish the integrity of the self-recording? A percentage of spot checks over total self-recordings on a time sampling could be used, for example, 50%, 80%, and so forth. Further, what types of consequences are needed for inaccurate recordings in order to establish accurate self-recordings over a lengthy period of maintenance? For example, does simple feedback on mistakes in self-monitoring result in accurate student recording of behavior? This could be tested in a reversal design by alternating feedback only with a feedback plus response cost contingency for error rates (see Table 5.7).

Comparing a number of management techniques with self-monitoring might constitute a valuable contribution to the research literature. For example, students whose behavior has led to suspensions might be good candidates for a study comparing suspensions and

Table 5.7

| REVERSAL DESIGN STUDY | | | | |
| --- | --- | --- | --- | --- |
| **BASELINE** | **FEEDBACK ONLY** | **FEEDBACK PLUS RESPONSE COST** | **REVERSAL** | **FEEDBACK PLUS RESPONSE COST** |
| Effect on rate of target behavior | ■ Rate of target behavior | ■ Rate of target behavior | Same as prior conditions | Same as prior conditions |
| | ■ Error rates | ■ Error rates | | |

self-monitoring. Other test conditions to compare might be weekly counseling, meetings with the principal, or behavioral procedures with reinforcement contingencies externally determined.

## SIT AND WATCH (TIME OUT)

### Suggested Readings

Cipani, E. (2008). *Classroom management for all teachers: Plans for evidence-based practice*. Upper Saddle River, NJ: Pearson Education.

Foxx, R. M., & Shapiro, S. T. (1978). The time-out ribbon: A nonexclusionary time-out procedure. *Journal of Applied Behavioral Analysis, 11*, 125–136.

Mace, F. C., Page, T. J., Ivancic, M. T., & O'Brien, S. (1986). Effectiveness of brief time-out with and without contingent delay. *Journal of Applied Behavior Analysis, 19*, 79–86.

Pinkston, E. M., Reese, N. J., LeBlanc, J. M., & Baxter, D. M. (1973). Independent control of a preschool student's aggression and poor interaction by contingent teacher attention. *Journal of Applied Behavior Analysis, 6*, 115–124.

White, A. G., & Bailey, J. S. (1990). Reducing disruptive behaviors of elementary physical education students with sit and watch. *Journal of Applied Behavior Analysis, 23*, 353–359.

### Brief Description

Sit and watch, also known as contingent observation, is a useful procedure for targeting problem behaviors in elementary grade level children during activities that are inherently pleasant for most students. Activities such as recess, playground activities, waiting for the bus home, and similar preferred school activities are well suited to the use of this procedure to reduce target problem behaviors. Sit and watch can be an effective consequence for disruptive, aggressive, or inappropriate behaviors during such activities. It targets specified problem behaviors on large groups of students through the contingent removal of the offending student from the naturally reinforcing activity. The removal is for a designated period of time.

## Procedures for Implementation

1. Identify target behavior(s) in the setting or context of interest.
2. Contingent upon the occurrence of the target behavior(s), the student is removed from the activity. He or she is asked to go "sit and watch" on a bench, on a chair, or in another area away from the activity until a timer (e.g., an oven timer) signals the end of such a period.
3. The student rejoins the activity after sit and watch.
4. Backup procedures for implementation can include the following:
   a. Go to sit and watch once during a day—lose daily computer time
   b. Go to sit and watch more than once during a day—lose a free play period
   c. Engage in disruptive behavior while in sit and watch—lose free play time later in the same day

## Hypothetical Example of Implementation: Roughhousing

The principal decides there is too much roughhousing in the elementary playground and decides to institute a sit-and-watch policy. After defining the specific behaviors that constitute roughhousing, the principal collects baseline data by having the playground supervisors record each incident. They write which roughhousing behavior occurred in a scoring code and the offender's initials on the recording sheet. The playground supervisors are told to scan the playground frequently for such occurrences. Following the collection of baseline data, the playground supervisors are instructed to immediately identify the target behavior and select the party or parties for sit and watch from a bench near the school building for a 3-minute period. If a student goes more than once to the sit and watch bench, he or she loses the remaining time in the recess as well as the following recess period.

## Demonstration Research Studies

The literature on time out, contingent observation, and sit and watch is fairly extensive. Replication studies may be needed in certain context areas or grade levels. However, the other types of applied research would prove a more unique contribution to the empirical literature for someone conducting research for a thesis or dissertation.

## Comparative Research Studies

What is probably lacking is a comparison of sit and watch with other, more common approaches to solving problem behavior(s) during everyday schoolchild-preferred activities. For example, very often infractions are first handled by the playground supervisor talking with the student about the offense. Possibly a second offense results in some form of removal. This could be tested against a consistent use of sit and watch with the backup contingencies specified above. The ABAB design in Table 5.8 illustrates such a study.

Other procedures that could be tested against sit and watch include detention, suspension, and counseling sessions. The school may be unwilling or unable to drop these procedures for implementation. Therefore the experimental design would have to have such procedures remain in effect throughout the study, with sit and watch added on during the B phases, allowing a comparison between current procedures and current procedures plus sit and watch. To ensure consistent implementation of sit and watch, some feedback to playground supervisors on their accuracy of implementing the procedure will probably be needed. Then the reversal condition would remove such feedback, probably making sit and watch a haphazard contingency in that condition (Table 5.9).

Table 5.8

| POTENTIAL STUDY: SIT AND WATCH | | | |
| --- | --- | --- | --- |
| (A) Baseline: Present procedures, which include haphazard use of sit and watch along with lectures | (B) Sit and watch | (A) Return to baseline | (B) Sit and watch |

Table 5.9

## EFFICACY OF SIT AND WATCH EXPERIMENTALLY TESTED

| Experimental condition | Condition A: Current strategies (e.g., visits with principal, counseling sessions) | Condition B: In addition to strategies used in A, sit and watch added | Condition A: Replicate prior A, i.e., remove consistent use of sit and watch | Condition B: Replicate prior B |
|---|---|---|---|---|
| Data collection | Collect data on target behaviors under current conditions | Collect data on target behaviors under existing strategies and addition of sit and watch | | Same as prior B condition |
| Possible effect on data | Baseline data | Behavior changes in desirable direction | Rate of behavior returns to baseline levels | Behavior changes again in desired direction, which demonstrates that desired results are obtained only when sit and watch is in effect[a] |

[a]You may then want to convince school personnel to drop their prior strategy; show data regarding the ineffectiveness of this strategy.

It might be better to implement a multiple baseline design across different supervisors, if you have one set on Tuesday and Thursday and another set on the other 3 days of the week. This would negate any spill-over effects. Another great comparison could be with those students who are on particular psychopharmacological medications for their behavior. The design would have to be the same as the prior design, allowing the medication to be provided throughout the study, as you may have no control over its use. However, demonstrating that a significant effect accrues only when sit and watch is deployed would provide a reason to question the continued use of the medication. It may also be the case that sit and watch for some students adds little to the effect of the medication, in which case you would show that behavior does not change across conditions (Table 5.10).

Table 5.10

**RELATIVE EFFECTS OF MEDICATION VERSUS SIT AND WATCH**

| Condition A: | Condition B: | Condition A: | Condition B: |
| --- | --- | --- | --- |
| Medication and current procedures | In addition to strategies used in A, sit and watch added | Replicate prior A | Replicate prior B |

The drawback of this type of medication study is the possibility that the medication is not given as prescribed. In many cases, medications may not be given every day or according to the dosing schedule dictated by the prescription order. In that case it would be hard to discern the effects.

Again, it may be difficult to get a true comparison of sit and watch with another strategy, especially if the alternate strategy is currently being deployed. However, with the use of a reversal design, you can add the sit and watch procedure during the B conditions to produce a cause-and-effect design. You may then demonstrate that the prior strategies resulted in rates of behavior that were not desirable (according to the data under A conditions). Only when sit and watch is added does behavior change.

## Parametric Studies

There is a great need to evaluate behavioral contingencies in terms of the effectiveness of these under less than consistent delivery. This is particularly true for the time out literature, although there are a few studies that have looked at this. How often do you hear that time out does not work? It is often because the implementation is poor. Parametric studies that examine implementation levels are very important in determining the conditions under which such a procedure is rendered ineffective.

For example, a parametric study might involve a comparison of the dependent variable of sit and watch at 100% implementation (i.e., for each occurrence) with 50% implementation (i.e., for every other occurrence). Of course, different parametric analyses than these can be selected, which answers the basic question, "How inconsistent can you be in using sit and watch and still get a behavioral effect?"

## RESPONSE CARDS

### Suggested Readings

Armendariz, F., & Umbreit, J. (1999). Using active responding to reduce disruptive behavior in a general education classroom. *Journal of Positive Behavioral Interventions, 1,* 152–158.

Cavanaugh, R. A., Heward, W. L., & Donelson, F. (1996). Effects of response cards during lesson closure on the academic performance of secondary students in an earth science course. *Journal of Applied Behavior Analysis, 29,* 403–405.

Christie, C. A., & Schuster, J. W. (2003). The effects of response cards on student participation, academic achievement, and on-task behavior during whole-class math instruction. *Journal of Behavioral Education, 12,* 147–165.

Gardner, R., Heward, W. C., & Grossi, T. A. (1994). Effects of response cards on student participation and academic achievement: A systematic replication with inner-city students during whole-class science instruction. *Journal of Applied Behavior Analysis, 27,* 63–71.

Narayan, J. S., Heward, W. L., Gardner, R., Courson, F. H., & Omness, C. K. (1990). Using response cards to increase student participants in an elementary classroom. *Journal of Applied Behavior Analysis, 23,* 483–490.

### Brief Description

The response card technique enables the teacher to monitor student performance in a variety of content areas (Armendariz & Umbreit, 1999; Cavanaugh, Heward, & Donelson, 1996; Christie & Schuster, 2003; Gardner, Heward, & Grossi, 1994; Narayan, 1990). The teacher presents a short oral lesson or assigns seat work and then checks the students' knowledge of the content. The teacher monitors comprehension by posing a series of questions to all the students in the class. All the students respond in the response card procedure, by writing brief answers on their dry erase boards. After a few seconds the teacher says, "Show your answers." The students hold up their answers for the teacher to survey. The teacher identifies those students who may be unclear about the material or readings. In contrast to the more traditional approach, in which one person is called on to answer, all the students respond to each question or item. Therefore, the teacher can determine whether most of the students have acquired the skills being taught using this technique.

The response card system requires a fair amount of work before delivering the lesson. The teacher or designer must identify the area of content that will be taught, then divide this area into small, teachable chunks. Subsequently, and most importantly, test items (questions that measure the objectives of the chunk of the total lesson) have to be generated. Obviously, each student in the class must have a clear writing surface, such as a dry erase board with a dry erase pen.

## Procedures for Implementation

1. Identify the content or class period in which the response card system will be used.
2. Delineate the chunks of material to be presented and the test items corresponding to each chunk.
3. Give each student a writing surface, for example, a dry erase board and a dry erase pen.
4. Explain the response card system to the students, and depending on their age have a few simple dry runs with easy material (i.e., several grade levels below their current level).
5. Present the chunk of material for the oral lesson or the assignment.
6. After the lesson presentation or seat assignment, have the students retrieve their writing surface and begin asking the test questions.
7. Give the students a few seconds to write their answers on their dry erase boards, then signal them to show their answers.
8. Scan the answers of all the students.
9. Present the correct answer to the class, praising a few students who gave the correct answer.
10. If too many students made errors, present the item again.
11. Continue this testing format until most students are demonstrating mastery, or revise the instructional method, lesson, or chunk of material.

## Hypothetical Example of Implementation: Use of Response Cards Following Seat Work

A seventh-grade teacher designates a reading assignment for the American history class. She designates the pages the students are to read within a certain amount of time in class. When they are done, the teacher poses questions about the content and the students are given a few seconds to respond, using their dry erase boards. The teacher then signals the class to show their answers. All students show their answers and the teacher scans the class, checking each student's answer. If a fair number of students miss certain items, she pinpoints the area in the reading that the question was based on and has them briefly read it again.

## Hypothetical Example of Implementation: Use of Response Cards During Lesson

A fifth-grade teacher is using response cards for her math instruction period. She provides a brief lesson on the new skill to be acquired by the students. During the lesson, she explains what the students are learning, and she provides a demonstration of the steps needed to solve the problem and a few examples with unison rehearsal. Subsequently she provides the students in pairs with items for them to respond to. Here is one of her sample lessons on teaching students to add mixed numbers with unlike fractions.

**Teacher:** OK, class, today we are going to learn how to add mixed numbers with unlike denominators. Here is a mixed number, three and a quarter. [Writes that number on the response board.] Let's add another mixed number to that, five and two sixths. [Writes that on her board.] Now watch me. We first convert the fractions in each number to a lowest common denominator, that being 12ths. Now what does three and one quarter converted to 12ths equal? Yes, 39/12ths. Now we do the same for the other mixed number, and we come up with 66/12ths. We can now add these two together to arrive at our answer, which is 105/12ths, and when we simplify this improper fraction back to a mixed number we get eight and 9/12ths or eight and three quarters. OK, now you try one. Get out your response boards. I want you to add five and a half to three and two thirds. Write on your scratch paper and then write your final answer on your response board.

**Class:** [Students copy down the problem on scratch paper and after about a minute, the teacher asks them to show their answers. Almost everyone missed the correct answer.]

**Teacher:** [Senses that the students did not fully grasp all the steps of this complex set of operations, so she decides to break it down. In particular, many were unable to convert the mixed number correctly.] OK, let's do just the first part of this problem, deriving the common denominator for unlike fractions. Let's add one quarter and two sixths. We first convert the fractions to the lowest common denominator, that being 12ths. Now we convert each fraction to its equivalent in 12ths. Watch while I show you the process again. [Teacher demonstrates process on one quarter and two sixths.] OK, your turn, try these two fractions. (Writes one third plus two fifths on her response board. Proceeds to give students about half a minute to solve that problem.) Ready, show.

**Class:** (All the students hold up their response board, with everyone getting the correct answer.)

**Teacher:** OK, let's try another one. Add one quarter plus two thirds. [Teacher waits and then repeats the process with this component of the skill until students are mastering this part.]

**Teacher:** [After eight items of just unlike fractions, she now adds the mixed number part.] Now let's go back and add mixed numbers with unlike fractions. [Demonstrates the procedure, having the students convert whole numbers into fractional parts of the lowest common denominator first and then having them convert the unlike fractions part. In other words, she makes this problem into a three-part problem: convert whole number, then convert unlike fractions, then add all of them together.]

By using response cards, the teacher finds that she is able to discern quickly whether she needs to provide more demonstrations or break the skill down even further. All students participate in the lesson now, in contrast to the previous situation, where she was not sure who was attending and who was not. Response cards have made the teacher more adept at meeting the students' needs for teaching.

## Demonstration Research Studies

A review of the existing literature might suggest the need for additional research studies assessing the efficacy of response cards at various grade levels, with different types of academic content, and within certain skills in the content areas. For example, it might be useful to conduct a study demonstrating the effectiveness of response cards in teaching students to factor a quadratic equation, particularly those students who were not amenable to previous attempts. As another example, how well can response cards work in teaching students to locate states and capital cities on a map, when compared with traditional approaches such as lecture, or independent seat work? The number of different areas of investigation is extensive at this point in the validation of this methodology.

Additional demonstration studies can test the efficacy of the paired-peer approach as well as true–false response mechanisms. For example, can using a true–false responding format develop skills that will translate to items that are multiple choice or short answer? Only research studies that test those items as generalization measures (in addition to true–false test items) will be able to answer that question empirically.

## Comparative Research Studies

Potential research testing other teaching and instructional procedures against response cards might be drawn from what the target students have already been exposed to. For example, a comparative study might be designed testing response cards against independent seat work on reading comprehension scores.

Table 5.11 provides a pictorial representation of this potential study. The first row depicts the experimental condition (i.e., ABAB). The second row delineates the experimental procedures for implementation, either baseline, which involves implementing the current teaching strategies (A), or the response cards procedure (B). The last row depicts the resulting data, demonstrating a change in behavior as a function of change in conditions.

## Component Analysis Research Studies

How important is feedback on correct answers? How important is the student presenting his or her answer for each test item? Some teachers who use dry erase boards defeat the utility of the response cards by just having the students write on them, as they would do with paper

Table 5.11

| POTENTIAL STUDY OF RESPONSE CARDS | | | |
| --- | --- | --- | --- |
| Condition A: Current strategies (seat work, long lecture, combination) | Condition B: Daily use of response cards in targeted content area | Condition A: Replicate prior A | Condition B: Replicate prior B |

Table 5.12

## RELATIVE EFFICACY OF RESPONSE CARDS WITH TEACHER-MONITORING COMPONENT

| Experimental condition | Condition A: Response cards with teacher monitoring | Condition B: Dry erase board, no teacher monitoring | Condition A: Replicate prior A | Condition B: Replicate prior B |
|---|---|---|---|---|
| Data collection | Collect data on attending behavior (on task) and performance on daily quizzes | Collect data on attending behavior (on task) and performance on daily quizzes | Collect data on attending behavior (on task) and performance on daily quizzes | Collect data on attending behavior (on task) and performance on daily quizzes |
| Possible effect on data | Baseline data | Behavior changes in desired direction | Rate of behavior returns to baseline levels | Behavior changes again in desired direction |

and pencil. These teachers do not incorporate teacher monitoring of the answers. Theoretically, this may prove ineffective because some students may require the monitoring in order to perform and attend. Additionally, the biggest factor is that the loss of the monitoring data does not allow the teacher to adjust his or her instruction as a function of student learning during the lesson. A reversal design depicts such a study (Table 5.12).

## REFERENCES

Armendariz, F., & Umbreit, J. (1999). Using active responding to reduce disruptive behavior in a general education classroom. *Journal of Positive Behavioral Interventions, 1*, 152–158.

Bailey, J. S., & Bostow, D. E. (1981). *Research methods in applied behavior analysis.* Tallahassee, FL: Copy Grafix.

Cavanaugh, R. A., Heward, W. L., & Donelson, F. (1996). Effects of response cards during lesson closure on the academic performance of secondary students in an earth science course. *Journal of Applied Behavior Analysis, 29*, 403–405.

Christie, C. A., & Schuster, J. W. (2003). The effects of response cards on student participation, academic achievement, and on-task behavior during whole-class math instruction. *Journal of Behavioural Education, 12*, 147–165.

Clark, H. B., Rowbury, T., Baer, A. M., & Baer, D. M. (1973). Timeout as a punishing stimulus in continuous and intermittent schedules. *Journal of Applied Behavior Analysis, 6*, 443–456.

Narayan, J. S., Heward, W. L., Gardner, R., Courson, F. H., & Omness, C. K. (1990). Using response cards to increase student participants in an elementary classroom. *Journal of Applied Behavior Analysis, 23*, 483–490.

Nelson, J. S., Alber, S. R., & Gordy, A. (2007). Effects of systematic error correction and repeated readings on the reading accuracy and proficiency of second graders with disabilities. *Etc, 27*, 186–198.

# Appendix A

# Reliability Formulas, Interobserver Agreement

## FREQUENCY DATA

Divide the smaller count by the larger count. For example, if observer D.S. records 15 occurrences of the target behavior while observer R.T. records 20 occurrences in the same reliability check, interobserver agreement is 15/20 = 75%.

## DURATION DATA

Divide the shorter record of cumulative duration for the session by the longer duration. For example, if the first observer records occurrences of the target behavior lasting 1 minute 20 seconds (80 seconds), while the second observer records 2 minutes 30 seconds in the same reliability check (150 seconds), interobserver agreement is 80/150 = 53.3%.

## INTERVAL RECORDING

Interval by interval agreement for occurrences and nonoccurrences entails determining the number of intervals for which both observers recorded the target behavior, divided by the total number of intervals. For example, if there are 80 total intervals, and the two observers agree on the scoring in 60 of them, the number of total agreements to disagreements is 60/80 or 75%.

Cooper, Heron, and Heward (2007, pp. 113–121) provide a more extensive delineation of interobserver agreement formulas.

## REFERENCE

Cooper, J. O., Heron, T. F., & Heward, W. L. (2007). *Applied behavior analysis* (2nd ed.). Columbus, OH: Merrill/Prentice Hall.

# Raw Frequency Data for Figure 3.1

| SESSION | FREQUENCY (DISPLAYED IN FIGURE 3.1) | SESSION | FREQUENCY (DISPLAYED IN FIGURE 3.1) |
|---|---|---|---|
| 1 (Baseline) | 0 | 16 (Reversal) | 3 |
| 2 | 0 | 17 | 2 |
| 3 | 1 | 18 | 1 |
| 4 | 0 | 19 | 1 |
| 5 | 1 | 20 | 1 |
| 6 | 1 | 21 | 2 |
| 7 (Praise) | 9 | 22 | 3 |
| 8 | 10 | 23 (Praise) | 11 |
| 9 | 12 | 24 | 11 |
| 10 | 12 | 25 | 12 |
| 11 | 12 | 26 | 11 |
| 12 | 11 | 27 | 12 |
| 13 | 13 | 28 | 11 |
| 14 | 10 | 29 | 11 |
| 15 | 10 | 30 | 13 |

# Graphing Data: General Rules for the *X, Y* Coordinate Plane

- The *x* axis marks time, and the length of time between each session, day, or week should be equidistant.
- The label for the *x* axis should appear horizontally below the *x* axis, for example, Sessions, Days, Weeks, and so forth.
- It is customary to not designate each *x* value on the axis; rather, groups of 5 or 10 are designated with a number that appears below the appropriate hash mark, for example, numbered sessions are 1, 5, 10, 15, and so forth.
- The *y* axis marks the dependent variable in the quantity measured, for example, frequency, duration, or percentage. Each unit should be equidistant; for example 10%, 20%, and 30% should be the same distance from each other.
- The label for the *y* axis should appear vertically and to the left of the *y* axis, for example, Percentage (%) Correct, Frequency of Tantrums, and so forth.
- Data points are plotted as a function of the session (*x* axis) and the value of the dependent variable (*y* axis) for that session.
- A data point is usually represented by a circle (open or closed). Other geometric forms such as a triangle or square may be needed in graphing the different conditions in the multielement design, depending on how many conditions there are, as each condition within the multielement design should be immediately visually apparent.
- Data points within each condition are connected by a line, either solid or dotted.
- Conditions are separated by a dotted line, and data points are not connected between conditions.

- Each baseline and experimental condition is labeled at the top of the graph in the appropriate condition.
- The figure is numbered in sequence as it appears in the manuscript and has a caption describing the variables involved.

# Raw Frequency Data for Figure 3.3

| SESSION | % OFF-TASK BEHAVIOR |
|---------|---------------------|
| 1 | 20 |
| 2 | 55 |
| 3 | 70 |
| 4 | 60 |
| 5 | 65 |
| 6 | 75 |
| 7 | 58 |
| 8 | 65 |

# Index